God is Not a Catholic

A Recovery Journey

for Adult Children of Parochial Schools

Endorsements for
God is Not a Catholic:

"Finally a book that teaches us how to heal in our own way....no cookie cutter plans here! Be sure to complete the inventories in the Appendix; this is how we personalize the information. The author's gentle, humor-filled style of writing shows us that she 'walks the talk' as she shares her own journey of forgiveness and the journey of others as they 'unlock their own hearts.'"

DIANE DETWILLER-ZAPP, MA, LPC, PRIVATE PRACTICE, PARADISE VALLEY/WICKENBURG, AZ. CO-AUTHOR OF *LAY CAREGIVING*.

"Dianne Pela's book, *God Is Not a Catholic* offers a healing pathway to those who were scarred by shame based discipline in parochial schools. Until Dr. Spock, the idea of 'spare the rod, spoil the child' was the prevailing social attitude regarding child rearing. Dianne's book is a primer for anyone who had shame or humiliation used as tools to enforce discipline."

KATHLEEN GARAST, RN, MA, DIRECTOR OF MARKETING AND DEVELOPMENT, ARIZONA ECUMENICAL INSTITUTE FOR SPIRITUAL DIRECTORS. FOUNDER, GARAST AND COMPANY CONSULTING.

"*God Is Not a Catholic* is an informative and entertaining read. Although the subject is serious, Ms. Pela writes with humor and wit, allowing the reader to gently hear its important message, work through many self-reflective exercises and ultimately, to move toward hope and healing."

ANNA VALENTI-ANDERSON, LCSW, LISAC, CSAT. FOUNDER, SANERESOURCES.ORG. CLINICAL DIRECTOR, CROSSWINDS COUNSELING SERVICES

"Dianne Pela's book is a gift of understanding, healing, and redemption for anyone who has experienced physical, emotional, sexual, or spiritual abuse. Dianne's ability to guide this healing comes from her own personal journey through pain, arriving at restoration and forgiveness. As a psychotherapist she has dedicated herself to the research and development of the treatment and path to healing outlined in her book. *God Is Not a Catholic* serves to reduce shame and address trauma from a place of grace and forgiveness. I highly recommend this powerful book!"

Sarah Matheson, MA, MA, LPC, private practice,
Scottsdale, AZ.

"In this incredibly courageous work, Ms. Pela shares her very personal journey to reclaim her authentic self and innovative guidelines to promote healing for the reader to do likewise. I consider this a powerful resource for anyone who has experienced humiliation and shame from the religious school experience. It is definitely on my list of recommended reading for clients."

Pat Pollard, MS, LPC, private practice,
Phoenix/Glendale, AZ.

"Dianne Pela has done an excellent job of laying out a recovery plan for healing childhood trauma. She illustrates the effects of abuse, through her own story as well as the stories of others, making the parochial school experience personal and easier to understand. She focuses on forgiveness as central to the healing process and her exercises in this area are particularly powerful. This book is an insightful and practical addition for professionals as well as for people struggling with their own abuse experiences."

Susanne C. Johnson, MA, LPC, private practice,
Carefree, AZ.

"I am also a product of parochial schools. Dianne has depicted the experience with accuracy, depth and courage. This is a must read for anyone who has endured the shame and guilt of the parochial school institution."

Anne McQuaid, MA, LPC, private practice,
Phoenix, AZ.

Dianne M. Pela, MA, LPC

God is Not a Catholic

A Recovery Journey for
Adult Children of Parochial Schools

Copyright © 2012 by Dianne M. Pela. *All rights reserved.* No part of this publication may be reproduced, distributed or transmitted in any form or by any means, including photocopying, recording or other electronic or mechanical methods, without the prior written permission of the publisher, except in the case of brief quotations embodied in critical reviews and certain other noncommercial uses permitted by copyright law. For permission requests, write to the publisher: info@lifeempowermenttherapy.com .

Intellectual Property Protection: The therapeutic concepts of LifeDanceTherapy© 2000 by Dianne Pela, MA, LPC are a merger of two pre-existing standard modalities—Neurolinguistic Programming and Therapeutic Dance. The resulting concepts extrapolated from such a merger are the sole property of Dianne M. Pela, MA, LPC and are protected under copyright law. Reproduction in any form without written consent is strictly prohibited. All copyrighted works are protected by United States Copyright Law (Title 17, United States Code) and the Berne Convention for the international protection of literary and artistic works. Federal and International Copyright protection laws extend to original and modified derivative models and concepts, and is applicable to intentional and unintentional infringements, and provides for specific statutory damages both civil and criminal.

Published by
Life Empowerment Therapy Publications
7558 W. Thunderbird Road #103
Peoria, AZ 85381

www.lifeempowermenttherapy.com

Cover design concept created by Dianne Pela
Cover Illustration by Terry Gomez-Sandoval
Cover lay-out by Duke Getzinger
Photography by Gordon Parlova and Mark Ericson

Printed in the United States of America
ISBN: 978-0-9857245-0-4
Library of Congress Control Number: 2012910446

ISBN: 978-0-9857245-1-1 ebook form

Library of Congress Cataloging in Publication Data pending

To Nick and Mary Pela for years of nurturing.

To Ron, Marianna, Erica and Scott for adding immense joy and happiness to my life.

Contents

Introduction   xiii

Part I: Organizing our Inner Resources

I.   Why Sister Mary Discipline Can't Get You Anymore 3

II.   Establishing Our Goals. 11

III.   Breaking the Denial. 27

IV.   Awareness and Yearning as Resources for Healing 41

V.   Understanding as a Resource for Healing. 59

VI.   You're Too Old to Play Victim Anymore:
Formula for Getting Rid of Victim Thinking 89

Part II. Healing Through Forgiveness of the Past

VII.   Your Personal Strategy for Forgiving:
What to do with the Feelings 109

Epilogue: God's Pure Child: Back to the Innocence 129

Chapter by Chapter Outline. 133

Appendices I -V 139

Index 169

References 171

Acknowledgments 173

About the Author 175

Author's Notes

This book is not about Catholic bashing. Rather, it is a call to forgiveness of the parochial school system of our past.

The book itself, together with the independent study which preceded it, has been completed since 1998. Updates and revisions were added in 2012.

The names of the "adult children of parochial schools" who have chosen to share information, as well as the names of the nuns and priests involved, have been changed.

The terms *parochial school, religious school,* and *Catholic school* are used interchangeably within the text of this book.

Introduction

In the early years of the parochial school system, shame, guilt, and fear were utilized as teaching tools and were instilled into children by the nuns and priests who taught them. Depending on several variables, many of these children took on and carried these insecurities into adulthood and are now experiencing physical illness, depression, and a wide array of self-defeating behaviors and shortcomings as a result.

How to experience successful recovery from having had an adverse childhood experience in a parochial school is an issue that needs addressing. Moreover, the particular method presented as a means of tapping into our inner resources for healing is crucial to recovery.

The main focus of *God Is Not A Catholic: A Recovery Journey for Adult Children of Parochial Schools* is recovery of these past traumas through awareness, enlightenment and forgiveness. To this end, a sharing of the stories of others who have gone through similar experiences (gleaned from an extensive independent study conducted among adult children of the religious school system) is presented. This sharing will lead to breaking the isolation and loneliness which often characterizes a person who has gone through any juvenile trauma.

The ultimate goal of the book is a move toward forgiveness of the transgressors, which is necessary in order to move on. **It is not about Catholic bashing.** Further, it is not a sensationalistic approach but rather a catalyst for healing. The goal is not to throw stones but to call to mind the personal transgressions, share with others' experiences which will serve to break the denial, work through the grief, forgive, and put closure to the past.

God Is Not A Catholic pulls together four powerful dynamics: the dysfunction of the religious school system of our childhood as an area to be looked at and healed; Neurolinguistic Programming (a communications technology concerned with visual, auditory and kinesthetic sensory modes) as a modality for tapping into our inner resources for healing; Neurolinguistic Programming (NLP) as a tool for forgiveness; forgiveness as a tool for healing. Within the realm of the book, the reader is made aware of some very basic, albeit overlooked, inner resources which may be implemented for healing emotional wounds.

I have spent the past two decades as a theorist, psychotherapist, motivational speaker and as an NLP trainer. During the course of the first two years as an NLP trainer, I began to perceive that people who use their kinesthetic sensory mode (primarily experience the world through what they feel as opposed to what they see or hear) are more susceptible to abuse than people who lead visually or in an auditory manner. Taking it one step further, among the kinesthetic people, those who are more introverted and introspective (personality type known as Melancholy) are more apt to internalize the abuse and have a harder time dealing with it.

During the same time frame, using my knowledge of NLP, I also suspected that the strategy used (visual, auditory, or kinesthetic) by an individual to remember something from the past is also that individual's same strategy for forgiving the past. I reasoned that if this were true, then knowing a person's personal NLP strategy for remembering the past could assist them in knowing their personal strategy for forgiving someone in their life. This is why I've incorporated an experiential exercise for you to find your personal strategy for forgiving. I believe that once you know your own personal strategy for forgiving, it allows you to zero in on that specific sensory mode (visual, auditory, kinesthetic or a combination thereof) as an avenue for healing.

Deciding to put both theories to the test, I conducted an independent study in order to research a seminar on forgiveness using NLP. At the same time I realized a need among many of the general populace of adult children of religious schools for forgiveness in their lives. Thus, the seed was planted for this project.

In January, 1992, the study began in three phases. Phase I was a questionnaire circulated among adults who had attended a religious school at some point in their childhood. It concerned their experiences, either pleasant or adverse. Phase II was a profile given to the same people to determine their temperament (personality type) and leading sensory mode (visual, auditory, kinesthetic). The results of both phases would indicate to me whether my idea that preferred sensory mode, coupled with personality type, played a role in degree of internalization of abuse. To date, with documented statistics to support fact, hypothesis became theory. We find that in almost all cases, temperament and sensory mode together usually determine degree of internalization of abuse.

The results of the study also indicate to me that NLP coupled with knowledge of the temperaments can be used as a modality for healing. In the guided imagery and meditations used throughout the book, special concern is made for all three preferred sensory modes. These are rich with visual, auditory, as well as kinesthetic cues. The participant can then pick and choose whichever meditations work best for them.

Phase III consists of research which indicates that forgiveness could indeed be achieved by applying the same personal strategy used for remembering past experiences.

In the past several years, the media has brought to our attention many scandals pertaining to men and women coming forward after a whole lifetime of silence, to name names of nuns and priests who molested them as children. I believe the time has come for a universal healing. Healing cannot take place without forgiveness.

Part I
Organizing Our Inner Resources

Chapter I

Why Sister Mary Discipline Can't Get You Anymore

Chapter I
Why Sister Mary Discipline Can't Get You Anymore

I remember thinking how worldly she was, for a nun. She loved Almond Joy and Mounds bars and made it known that she liked it when anyone, especially the boys, brought them to her. She made subtle references to sex during classroom lessons. And, sometime during the first week of school, Sister Mary Luke had moved the desks. Instead of five rows of nine students, we now had three short rows of girls on one side of the room and three rows of boys on the other side of the room, with a large aisle in between. She told us, with a smirk on her face, that if we didn't already know why she was separating us, we soon would.

The tone of Sister's voice implied that we were in store for some sort of bad behavior. I felt dirty. I thought Sister Mary Luke was telling me it was bad to associate with boys. Now, over forty years later, I realize the serious social and sexual implications put upon my classmates and me by her innuendoes.

But in the fall of 1957, I was a naive twelve-year-old Catholic schoolgirl, trying hard to be the best reflection of God and my parents I could be.

As it was, I could have said two dozen rosaries a day and Sister wouldn't have cared. Sister didn't like me.

During the first week of school, two of the boys in our room had been fooling around on the playground and had broken my eyeglasses. My mother wrote a note to Sister, telling her about this. Sister took the two boys out into the hallway to talk to them and, when they denied the whole thing, Sister called me a liar in front of all my classmates. That entire year, whenever she called on me to answer a question, she would refer to me as "The Liar." She made it very apparent that she disliked me.

There was something else about Sister Mary Luke that didn't seem right to me. I remember thinking, "Sister likes Jeremy the way I like Brian." But that couldn't be! "She can't have a crush on Jeremy," I reasoned. "Nuns just don't do that."

I felt scandalized. But, by all indications, Sister liked Jeremy differently than her other pets. She sat him up front by her and would always talk to him throughout our weekly written spelling test. If I didn't know better, I'd swear she was giving Jeremy the answers!

During the course of the year, Sister managed to ostracize Jeremy from the rest of the class. All the other boys thought of him as "teacher's pet," although I don't know if they ever actually called him that. What I do know is that something happened on the playground one day and when we reassembled for class after recess, Sister Mary Luke asked all the boys who were "against Jeremy" to raise their hands. All the boys raised their hands. I felt so bad for Jeremy! I don't remember the rest of it, but I know it must have been very humiliating for him.

Thirty-three years later, at a class reunion, Jeremy told me the rest of his story. I was shocked and, as he talked about what had happened, my own memories and feelings of shame rushed back to me.

> "One of the nuns used to molest me," he told me. "She did it repeatedly throughout the entire school year. She said that if I didn't do what she wanted, she would punish the class. I felt a responsibility to the whole class. She used to keep me after class to 'help' her. My dad would come to pick me up afterward, and we would give her a ride back to the convent. They would be in the front seat and I'd be in the back seat, wishing we would all get into a car accident and be killed so I wouldn't have to deal with it anymore! I couldn't tell my

parents what was happening, and I felt horrible shame. I also felt misunderstood by my classmates. How could I tell them what she was doing to me?"

Jeremy's story is only one horrifying example of how children's lives can be scarred by nuns and priests who have molested them. Oftentimes in the early years of the parochial school system, shame, guilt and fear were utilized as teaching tools and were instilled in children by the nuns and priests who taught them. Depending on several variables, many of these children took on and carried these insecurities into adulthood and are now experiencing depression, physical illness, and a wide array of self-defeating behaviors.

In the past twenty years, more and more media coverage has been given to stories of men and women who were sexually abused as children by priests and nuns. After a whole lifetime of silence, these former children of religious schools are dealing with the memories of these molestations. The fact that the silence is being broken is good news. And, now that we've identified these adverse childhood experiences in parochial school, it's time for healing to take place. And healing cannot take place without forgiveness.

Chances are, if you've picked up this book, you're one of many people who haven't yet recovered from an unpleasant parochial school experience. It took me a while to reconcile my own similar feelings, and I wrote ***God Is Not a Catholic: A Recovery Journey for Adult Children of Parochial Schools*** with the intention of helping others recover from similar past traumas. There are others like you, and their stories appear in these pages to help you feel less alone in your struggles to get through the feelings.

FORGIVENESS AS A TOOL FOR HEALING

This book is not about Catholic bashing! I, myself, was very anti-Catholic for many years before I realized that I was the one losing out. Harboring resentment against the Catholic Church and school system was keeping me locked into very bitter feelings. In my journey toward closing the door on the past, I found that I had to take a giant leap toward forgiveness of my transgressors in order to move on. I would like to share with you what I learned along that road to forgiveness.

Toward that end, ***God Is Not a Catholic: A Recovery Journey for Adult Children of Parochial Schools*** employs three powerful dynamics while facing the dysfunction of the religious school system of our childhood: Neurolinguistic Programming (NLP), a concept that addresses the way people experience the world; NLP as a tool for forgiveness; and forgiveness as a tool for healing. Within these pages, you'll be made aware of some basic inner resources for healing emotional wounds brought on by your childhood experiences.

The first dynamic mentioned, Neurolinguistic Programming, is a concept that people experience the world through one of three senses—sight, sound, or feeling. During the course of my work as an NLP trainer, I began to suspect that people who experience the world through what they feel are more susceptible to abuse than those who experience the world through sight or sound. I've noticed that, among these "feeling" people, many are more apt to internalize past abuse, or what they perceive as abuse, and have a harder time recovering from it. After some research, I began to suspect that personality type also plays a part in whether a person internalizes what he perceives as abuse. (Much more will be said about NLP and about the personality types later.)

In order to prove these two theories, I conducted an independent study of adult children of religious schools. I circulated a questionnaire among adults who had attended a religious school at some point in their childhood. The questionnaire inquired about their experiences, either pleasant or adverse. Later, a profile of the same people determined their personality type and manner of learning (through sight, sound or feeling). The results of both the study and the profile indicated to me that

Chapter I. Why Sister Mary Discipline Can't Get You Anymore

the way in which a person learns, as well as their personality type, influences whether or not a person will internalize abuse or what they perceive as abuse.

As I learned more about NLP, I reasoned that the memory strategy we use (either through sight, sound or feeling) to remember something from the past is the same strategy we use for forgiving the past. Therefore, knowing a person's personal strategy for remembering the past can assist them in knowing how best to forgive people who had wronged them. Consequently, **I found the secret to forgiving people in our lives:** it involves finding out how you, personally, remember things, based on your own personal strategy. Everyone does it differently, and you'll find out later on in this book what works best for you.

We can't heal from something unless we examine it, feel the pain, work through the emotions, and forgive our transgressors. The good news is that every one of us has within us what we need in order to forgive. These inner resources can take away our bitterness and resentment and bring us back to a fuller life. I found this out myself, in a place where I would never have imagined.

In the 1980's, during a time of intense self-discovery, I realized that a lot of my intense pain was coming from unresolved issues caused by the molestation that had taken place when I was seven by a girlfriend's brother. I was still carrying around guilt, shame and fear from that negative experience and had become spiritually dead inside. At that point, I did not feel confident that the faith I'd been indoctrinated into as a child, the Catholic faith, could offer any answers for me. After all, the things the nuns had told us about God translated into the image of a big, punitive Being, ready and more than willing to zap me into Hell!

By 1984, it must have been very obvious to my family that something was wrong. My brother John came to me one day and insisted I participate in a weekend retreat being held for divorced and widowed persons called Beginning Experience.

Now, my brother John is a very mild-mannered man. He had never *insisted* I do anything before, so he really got my attention. So much so that it only took me six months of procrastination before I was able to drive myself to my Beginning Experience weekend.

There, the punitive God of my youth was gone. The focus instead was on a loving and caring Father in Heaven. Instead of sermons about hellfire and brimstone, I heard only about ways in which to spread love and help people.

One of the many things I learned that weekend was the importance of forgiving for the sake of our healing, not for the sake of the transgressor. When we stubbornly refuse to forgive, we give away our power! Our transgressor still has power over our lives and THEY WIN. When we carry the burden of hatred, the pay-off to us is cynicism and a hardened heart. We cannot live life to the fullest because we have become embittered. Forgiveness can be the key to unlocking one's heart. My heart had been telling me all along that forgiveness was the key to my happiness, but I chose not to listen. The answer had been there all the time. It reminds me of one of my favorite books, *The Wonderful Wizard of Oz,* by Frank Baum. In the final pages, we see that the "wizard" directed Dorothy and Toto, Scarecrow, Lion and Tin Man to everything they had desired, but to nothing they did not already possess inside their hearts!

Many of you have also been diligently etching away at yourselves, trying to eliminate anything from your personality that isn't healthy. Perhaps you've tried self-help books and therapy sessions and are still coming up unhappy and sad, as I did. In that case, the missing road to wholeness may be in dealing with your childhood and/or present day experiences in a way that will allow you to forgive all of your transgressors. There is strength in looking at an issue in our lives that we've previously skirted.

In Chapter Two, I'll share with you my experience of forgiveness, and how rich the spiritual rewards were. Without that softening of my heart, I could have never effectively written this book.

Chapter I. Why Sister Mary Discipline Can't Get You Anymore

As part of my independent study for the book, I interviewed people with whom I had attended Catholic school in the small mid-western town where I was born and raised. I felt these people would be my most important sampling, since we'd had the same experiences at the hands of the same nuns. On a personal level, I'd cherished the faces of these children of long ago all my life, and dearly wanted to connect with them again as adults.

Of course, upon interviewing the people with whom I'd gone to parochial school, I got more than I had bargained for. After hearing Jeremy's story, I put down this project for almost two years. I was too horrified by what I'd heard, and afraid of what else I would uncover. Nuns molesting children was something I only had read about and had seen on television. But, in my own classroom? In an obscure way, every kid in that room had been emotionally molested when Sister Mary Luke told Jeremy, "If you don't do this, I'll punish the class."

Jeremy is the reason I had to follow through with this project. My sincere hope is that the stories and solutions in this book will help all the people like Jeremy who read it to resolve their anger and hurt and move forward with happy, successful lives.

Chapter II

Establishing Our Goals

Chapter II
Establishing Our Goals

ELEANOR'S STORY

Eleanor made me swear I wouldn't use her real name before she told me what the nuns did to her. "I'll only tell you if you promise to make up a different name for me," she said. "I never talk about this with anyone, not even my husband."

Then she began her story, a story I'd heard so many times before, and would hear many more times before my work was done:

> "The nun who was my fifth grade teacher was completely insane. I mean, Sister Marie Purgatoria (not her real name) wasn't quirky or a little different. This woman was mental ward material. Some of the things she made us do were so bizarre. First of all, we'd have to put our heads down on our desks, with our eyes closed. She called this 'nap time,' even though we were far too old to be taking naps. She'd come by each desk while our eyes were closed, and either give us a gold star on our open hand or a smack with the ruler. We'd never know which one was coming. Too often, I received a firm smack and I remember thinking that I must be a very bad person. What we'd get depended on whether she thought we were good or bad."

> "Other times, when our heads were down, she'd pick a name at random. That person would have to get up and go to her. The rest of the class wouldn't be allowed to peek. Sometimes we'd hear the ruler smacking flesh. Sometimes we'd hear shuffling. Sometimes only whispers back and forth. I was only picked once and I never peeked while any of my classmates were up there. But, when I was up there, she asked me if I wanted to kiss her or get an enema. I didn't even know what an enema was, so I said I'd kiss her. I kissed her on the cheek and she

put her tongue in my ear. It made me throw up. I threw up all over her black pointy shoes. She told everyone to raise their heads. Then, right in front of everyone, she cleaned her shoes on my uniform skirt. She wiped the vomit off my shoes with my school uniform, and I had to wear it the rest of the day. I don't know what other things she would have made me do if I hadn't thrown up. I thank God I threw up."

"I never told my parents about 'nap time.' Sister told us that this was for all kids everywhere and that our parents had to go through it. But, they never talked about it and would get very upset if they heard us talk about it. Sister Marie Purgatoria told us that it was part of growing up and it made you a better person. She once said that our parents had to pay extra for us to receive this 'nap time.' She said that if some of us weren't called up to her, it was because our parents couldn't afford it. So, we shouldn't talk about it to each other because we'd embarrass some of our classmates whose parents couldn't afford it. I wanted to tell my parents about all my torments, but my fourth grade nun had said we should bear our tribulations in silence, so I told no one."

Innocence and Sweetness

We were all born with loving innocence and sweetness which felt like springtime, looked like rows of pastel flowers, and sounded like a pan flute and a harp playing a duet. Remember? Somewhere in the recesses of your mind, you remember.

As we've grown, some of us have lost our loving innocence and that old feeling of sweetness through fear, trauma, addiction, or deprivation (not getting our needs met). Going back to reclaim this part of our personality has become a way of life for some of us. We've devoted our lives to getting rid of our toxic diets, applying the rules of positive thinking, or learning a multitude of pop psychology phrases.

As stated in Chapter I, I'd done an extensive amount of personal growth work on myself in the 1980's. I realized then that a lot of my pain was coming from my molestation at age seven.

Chapter II. Establishing Our Goals

However, a good deal of my torment had been a direct result of the guilt, shame and fear instilled in me by the nuns and priests of my parochial school days.

When I started conducting personal growth seminars twenty-five years ago, I met countless numbers of people who, like me, had gone to a parochial school. Ironically, many of them shared the same adverse feelings of guilt, shame and fear from growing up in that school system.

At around the same time, I began to notice that people in my Twelve-Step Codependents Anonymous meetings were talking more about the damage done to them in the name of God by the religious teachers of their past.

The process of recovering from spiritual abuse will sometimes be painful. But, as author and lecturer John Bradshaw has said many times, "you can't heal what you can't feel." Together, we will carefully examine areas of our lives which need healing. We will address each feeling as it emerges.

Our ultimate goal in this book is to learn how to forgive, at the time we are ready to forgive. We need to erase old memories from our religious school teaching that tell us that God wants us to forgive right away. One of the reasons God gave us a free will is so we could elect to use it for growth. And this growth should include not merely praying away transgressions against us, but also asking for the strength to grow as we face our pain.

There is so much written about forgiveness—but where does one start to learn how to forgive?

Neurolinguistic Programming: What is it and How it Can Help You Forgive

Neurolinguistic Programming is a buzz phrase from the 1980's self-help movement. You may already know the concept, even if you don't recognize the name. Put plainly, Neurolinguistic

Programming (NLP) is a concept that suggests that we all perceive the world differently. People primarily experience the world through one of three senses—sight, sound or feeling. Those of us who primarily collect our knowledge of the world around us through our sense of sight are visual people. People who relate to the world through the way things sound are auditory people. Kinesthetic people are those who lead with what they feel. (When someone says that he's going to "trust his gut instinct," you can be sure that he's coming from his kinesthetic mode.)

The way in which you are experiencing the world at any given time—through sight, sound, or feeling—is called your preferred sensory system. We all learn through one of, or a combination of, these three different sensory systems.

This is not to say that visual people always learn through their sense of sight, that auditory people always learn through their sense of hearing, or that kinesthetic people always learn best through "getting a feel" for things. But we do tend to favor one of the three, and can flip-flop back and forth throughout the course of a day, using different strategies for different things.

Let's say that you and a friend meet at the mall. When you part at the end of the day, your friend wants to give you his new phone number. Since neither of you brought anything to write with, you decide to memorize the phone number. How do you go about doing that? If you picture the numbers as he gives them to you and learn them by seeing the numbers in your mind's eye, then your strategy for remembering that phone number would be visual.

If, however, in order to memorize a phone number, you first say it to yourself and you actually hear your own voice repeating the number, this would be an auditory strategy, because you are learning by hearing.

And finally, let's say that when given a phone number to memorize, you get a "feeling of association," as if the number seems to go with that person. Or perhaps, upon dialing the

CHAPTER II. ESTABLISHING OUR GOALS

number, you "get a feeling" that you are dialing incorrectly. In that instance, you are leading kinesthetically.

Now is a good time to find your preferred sensory mode. Turn to Appendix III and take the test.

So, what did you find out about yourself on the test? Are you visual, auditory or kinesthetic? Or a combination? You probably want to save your results. Knowing what sensory mode you usually favor will be helpful later in this book. Just remember... we don't use one sensory mode exclusively. We use different modes for different tasks.

When I first learned about NLP, I'd been conducting seminars and workshops for about two years, primarily focusing on issues like *Healing the Child Within, Stress Management*, and *Mastering Your Life Through Positive Thinking*. I was using, and still use, a lot of guided imagery as a tool with which to achieve forgiveness as well as manage stress and conquer illness.

Guided imagery is a process by which the mind is transported to a different place than the body physically occupies. An example of guided imagery would be if I say to you, "Let your mind wander to a field of daisies. Allow yourself to see the daisies in your mind's eye." This is guided imagery because I am <u>guiding</u> you, by my words, to imagine something.

I'd always been careful to use auditory language ("<u>listen</u> to the <u>babbling</u> brook") kinesthetic language ("<u>feel</u> the <u>warm</u> rays of sun on your back") and visual language ("<u>see</u> the <u>magenta</u> sky after the sunset") whenever I created the relaxation techniques for the seminars in order to address all methods of learning. Back in the late 1980's, when I was producing guided imagery audio tapes to be used and sold in my seminars, I would double-check to make sure that I was addressing all three ways in which a person connects, before even going into the recording studio.

But now, here was a communications technology, NLP, which I could use to enhance my seminars. By knowing my participants' preferred sensory mode for completing a specific task, I could help them achieve their goals more quickly. And, I thought, why not use it as a modality for healing illness, for forgiveness, for all my seminars and private work with clients and patients?

NLP as a Modality for Remembering

Shortly after learning about NLP, I took a trip to Birmingham, Michigan, a suburb of Detroit. There I was, driving down the streets I hadn't seen in six years. I noticed that, as I came upon different houses, buildings, gas stations and other familiar points, I would first experience some very unsettling feelings in my stomach. Before I knew what the feelings were about, I started remembering the sound of the voices of different people associated with these places. Next, I got clear pictures of what had transpired at some of these places. It was clear to me that my personal strategy for remembering events which had transpired at a particular place was first kinesthetic (because I first got that "gut" feeling), then auditory (because of the voices I was reminded of), and finally visual (because of the images that then surfaced).

Using NLP to Help Heal Memories

I decided to use this knowledge of how I remember events which had transpired long ago to do more "Inner Child" healing work. So I drove the five hours to my birthplace in Ohio. My purpose was to confront the man who had molested me when he was a teenager and I was only seven years old.

I decided to pay a visit to the house where he had molested me. I knew that in order to heal my little girl persona, (that part of my psyche which was still reacting as a frightened seven year old girl would react), I would first have to remember everything. Because my strategy for remembering in a place I hadn't been in a long time was kinesthetic-to-auditory-to-visual, in that order, I concentrated on getting myself into the house where the molestations actually happened. I knew that if I could experience the place again, some of the old *feelings* that I had experienced then might come back (kinesthetic strategy for remembering). Subsequently, I knew that, since the family still lived there, actually *hearing* familiar voices could also jar memories (auditory strategy for remembering). And, if I were able to *see* how the house and people really were now (visual strategy for remembering) compared to how I had always recalled all of it, feelings that needed healing would surface.

During the four-hour car trip, I constantly addressed that part of my psyche who was still a frightened seven-year-old girl. I told her that we were going to pay a visit to Mitchell (not his real name). I said to her that we were going to let go of the shame. I reassured her that I would never let anyone hurt her again.

When I arrived in the neighborhood where I had lived when I was a child, I parked the car in front of my old house. I walked up the street and around the corner to the house that Mitchell's family still owned. I felt the entire experience would be more healing for me if I walked there, the way I used to when I was small.

On Mitchell's street, I passed the house that had caught fire and burned halfway to the ground shortly after Mitchell had started molesting me. The house had been restored after all these years, and I could tell by the name on the lamp-post that the same family still resided there.

When I was seven, I used to walk past that house with my arm covering my face as I was on my way to play with Mitchell's sister Sally (not her real name). I was scared to death that that house would "come alive" and get me for what I'd done. The fire that had consumed that house had been, for me, synonymous with Hell's fire. I was so consumed with unrealistic guilt that I had become deathly afraid that my own house would catch fire at night while my family and I slept. Many times during the night, I would sit up in bed to make sure I didn't smell smoke.

But now, halfway to Mitchell's old house, my thoughts shifted back to the present. My plan was to experience how I felt once inside the house where it had all happened. And I planned to ask Mitchell's parents where I might find him. Certainly, I had no intention of telling his parents, now in their seventies, what their son had done many years before. There was no point in that; I sought healing for myself, not retribution. Once I had Mitchell's address, I would confront him privately about what he had done.

But things did not happen as I'd planned. Instead, they happened just as fate would have them happen. Or maybe God had something to do with it. When Mitchell's father answered my knock at the door and I told him who I was, he greeted me with a smile. Remembering me as one of the girls who used to play with his daughter, he invited me in.

Imagine my surprise when I stepped into the living room and saw Sally, who was visiting from another state! We hugged. With great pride, she introduced me to her husband and small pre-school son. The irony of what happened next still amazes me! Sally nodded in the direction of a man and woman who were sitting in the far corner of the living room and asked, "Do you remember my brother Mitchell?"

So, there I was in the same living room where, many years before, Mitchell had forced Sally and me to take off our clothes. I knew that just upstairs was the room that had been Sally's bedroom, where he had forced us to play "doctor" while he masturbated. And just underneath us was the basement where, at Sally's seventh birthday party, and in the presence of at least seven other little girls, he had taken my hand and had forced me to masturbate him.

And because Mitchell had never tried to force intercourse, I spent many of my years discounting the episodes to myself. It was not until I began my undergraduate work in psychology that I realized what had happened was indeed a molestation.

Chapter II. Establishing Our Goals

And here I was in that living room with Mitchell, his wife, Sally, her husband, Sally's son, and Sally and Mitchell's parents! To do anything more than merely nod in the direction of Mitchell would have been terribly inappropriate. I couldn't help noting, however, how haggard and worn he now looked.

What was extremely healing was coming face-to-face with the man who had molested me. Everything fell into perspective for me at that moment. I was able to feel, hear and see that what had happened was in the distant past. He had been a boy of fifteen at the time and was now a man in his fifties. He wasn't the same person. My intuition told me that he had had a life filled with turmoil. I heard the pain in his voice and I saw the hurt and sadness in his eyes. The outcome of this confrontation was very healing for me.

Before Mitchell and his wife left the house, he turned to me and, without looking me in the eye, said, "are you one of those girls who used to hang around and give me a bad time?" He sounded a little sarcastic and I've always felt that he made the remark as a defense against the guilt that he'd been feeling.

I wanted to jump up and choke him! I wanted to tell him how much pain he had caused me as a child *and* as an adult! But, because other innocent people would be hurt by any such outburst from me, I did none of those things.

Instead, I let my little girl persona do it, kinesthetically. By that I mean, I visualized myself as a little girl, standing up to that man and yelling all the expletives at him that I could imagine: "What do you mean, I gave you a hard time? You molested me! You did a despicable thing and now I let go of that shame which I've been carrying around for you all of these years!"

What I *actually* said to him in reply I honestly don't remember. I may have given him a little smirk, with no verbiage at all. The important thing is that, while using the concepts involved in NLP, I was kinesthetically able to get out my anger, let go of Mitchell's shame that I'd been carrying around, and heal that part of my persona that needed healing.

I left that house shortly after Mitchell and his wife did. I cannot tell you what a relief I felt, as I walked up the street, and around the corner, back to the car! I felt like a thirty-year-old weight had been lifted from my shoulders. It had! Before I even realized what I was doing, I started swinging my arms, just like a carefree kid again! I suddenly felt hungry, and remembered an apple that I had tossed into my purse that morning for the trip. Reaching into my purse, I lifted the apple out and began tasting the sweetness of the fruit, letting the juices run down my arm as I ate.

As I passed by the house which had once burnt down, I paused a moment. I reflected on the symbolism of this beautiful restoration of a once fire-damaged house. To me, the house now represented how the ugly memories of one's past can be transformed into something strong and beautiful again. And I realized, while I looked at the house, that for the first time ever, I had faced the fire!

Using NLP as a Modality for Forgiveness

The emotional healing I experienced that day in 1990 when I let go of the shame I'd been carrying around from my childhood molester was just the beginning. After I returned home, I created a guided imagery exercise for myself which included some kinesthetic, auditory and visual language (in that order, because that is my personal strategy for remembering). I then audio-taped the guided imagery exercises to use for healing myself, and for forgiving Mitchell. (It was before the invention of the compact disc. I am, after all, old!) I believe that the same strategy we each use for remembering will also help us release and forgive.

In Part II of this book, I will share with you how you can find your own strategy for remembering and forgiving, to help you in your own healing process. We will focus on what NLP can do for you in coping with the demons in your life. I want to share with you what I have found to be true, both in my own life, with the participants in my seminars, and in assisting many clients and patients through the years: we can use NLP as a modality to help us forgive the violators in our life.

If you are experiencing that, no matter how you try and what you do, you cannot seem to forgive the people who need forgiving in your life, let me show you some new ways in which to achieve this, using your own personal strategy for forgiving. In other words, let's really zero in on things.

Make no mistake; there are no shortcuts. But it will be less discouraging if you know which road toward forgiveness to take, up front. This will be your personal map for forgiveness. It may be entirely different from anyone else's.

WHY FORGIVE?

You may be asking, "why forgive?" Maybe you were spiritually abused by the teachers you had in the religious school system, and made to think that everything you did was a serious sin. Maybe you feel as though you were spoon-fed guilt in the school cafeteria. I know I felt that the donuts and hot chocolate they served after communion every First Friday were laced with self-hate. I remember swallowing the donuts over a lump in my throat hot with what I thought were the fires of Hell. And as I sat stuffing down self-hatred, I just knew that God Himself would strike me dead and those hell-fires would consume me for the bad communion I just made. I remember that feeling of repressed guilt very well because I, like thousands of others, survived it.

Maybe the unspeakable was done to you. Maybe you were sexually molested by one of these so-called spiritual leaders. This is an ugly truth that's becoming harder to ignore. So-called "people of God" have molested innocent children. And if you were indeed one of these children whose innocence was taken away, you may be feeling that your perpetrator does not deserve forgiving.

So, why forgive? What's the payoff? It's simple: for you to be born anew, you must shed the heavy burden you have been carrying around all these years in order to experience a renewal of your former innocence. Along with that innocence comes peace of mind.

As badly as you want peace of mind, you may cling just as stubbornly to your self-righteous anger. After all, you might say, those people violated me terribly. I'm the wronged one and they deserve all the badness that I can imagine happening to them.

I personally shed a very heavy burden from my past and was able to forgive the nuns and priests for the spiritual abuse I had received. Fifteen years prior to becoming a licensed psychotherapist, I was introduced to a weekend recovery program called Beginning Experience, mentioned earlier. After my initial B. E. weekend, I was invited to become a peer counselor and facilitate future weekends with other peer counselors.

Beginning Experience (B. E.) is an international program that is instrumental in helping divorced and widowed people grow through their stages of grief. During the B.E. weekend, there is a reconciliation process. At one point, in ritualistic manner, a man, a woman, and a priest get up in front of everyone. The man represents the male spouse who may have left you through death or divorce. The woman, of course, represents the female spouse who may have left. And the priest represents the church system who may have, albeit unknowingly, committed transgressions against the B.E. participant. Each representative asks to be forgiven. The participant is invited to go up and make peace with the appropriate person.

This ritual, as many times as I'd facilitated a B.E. weekend, had always been a powerful tool with which I forgave several people in my life. But I never could go up to the priest. I felt really bitter and angry at the nuns and priests who I felt had helped ruin my childhood, and I wanted to hang onto that bitterness and anger, thank you very much.

Chapter II. Establishing Our Goals

However, while facilitating a B. E. weekend about a year after my initial weekend, one of the female participants in the group assigned to me whispered, "I really need to go up to the priest, but I'm scared. Would you go up with me?" Choking down the lump in my throat, I told her I would. Although I realized that the woman wanted me to merely accompany her as she walked up to the priest, I felt apprehensive.

I waited as the woman stood in front of the priest. As the priest, who was a representation of all priests and nuns, said to her, "forgive me," I could no longer keep back the tears which had been filling my eyes. As the woman started to hug the priest, I could see by her posture that something in her was being transformed. As she had walked up to the priest from her seat, with me behind her, her gait had been very stiff, almost robot-like. Now her entire stature had become softer, more relaxed. Her shoulders slumped, as though a heavy weight had been lifted, and she unlocked her knees. Even her tear-stained face had changed. Gone was the tight jaw, the firmly held mouth. In place of the tenseness, I saw joy.

By the time the woman finished hugging the priest, I knew what my heart was telling me to do. I stepped up to the priest and he became, for me, Sister Mary Luke, Sister Crissanna, Sister Carmella, (not their real names) and all the other nuns who had abused me spiritually, intellectually, and emotionally.

I don't know how long I stood hugging the priest after he asked me to forgive him. As I forgave all the nuns who had helped cause me such pain in my life, I felt as if years of callousness and hardness were dropping from me. I know that the time I spent with him changed my heart, and I haven't been the same since. I imagine that, at that moment, I felt very much what the Tin Man from the *Wizard of Oz* must have experienced when he felt his heart—the heart that he'd had all along—start beating.

Remember that God wants us to forgive, <u>when we're ready</u>. It may take years to do, and that's certainly all right. It's a journey which has several pitfalls along the way. But, if you dig deep enough and diligently enough, your rewards will be great.

Before my own reconciliation experience, I had been praying for peace of mind. I got it that day, but I first had to experience my feelings, embrace them, and then let them go. As I learned many years ago in Beginning Experience, the only way out of the pain is through. That is the way to stand and face the fire!

Chapter II. Establishing Our Goals

Things to Remember After Reading Chapter II:

- You're about to embark on a real journey.
- You've already begun the journey by picking up this book.
- It took a tremendous amount of courage to begin this journey.
- You are a courageous person!
- Courage is always rewarded.
- Treat yourself with respect for having this courage.
- Acknowledge that you will be using energy in order to work through feelings.
- Be very gentle with yourself while reading these chapters.
- Have regard for your tender humanity!

Affirmation for Chapter II:

"I am a very courageous person."

Chapter III

Breaking the Denial: Owning Our Experiences with the Parochial School System

Chapter III
Breaking the Denial: Owning Our Experiences with the Parochial School System

I've always believed there is a thin line between positive thinking and denial. Positive thinking is a form of thinking which accentuates the positive in any given situation, even an adverse one. Denial, on the other hand, is the act of saying "no" even when your spirit knows the truth. It's a disavowal that anything bad has happened.

Let's say that your spouse of twenty-two years, whom you dearly love, has just left you for another. You're nursing fresh wounds, since the separation just took place a month ago. When I call and ask how you're doing, you say that you're just fine. You actually think you mean that you're just fine, and that you are thinking positively. Actually, instead of dealing with any of your pain, you've gotten very busy at your workplace to unconsciously avoid dealing with your pain. Consequently, you're in denial that you're in any pain.

Sometimes we use self-abusive behavior to mask our pain. It was Carl Jung who said, "Neurosis is always a substitute for legitimate suffering."

In other words, instead of experiencing the suffering that we need to go through in order to heal, we engage in self-abusive behavior to mask our hurts. In doing so, we're using a form of denial.

Having had the experience of working as a psychotherapist in two world-renowned inpatient treatments centers, I can tell you that this is the sort of behavior that keeps mental health wards full. If you think that our culture's "crutches"—drugs, over-eating, alcohol, and excessive spending, gambling, sex or work—don't lead to stresses in our lives that can lead to breakdowns, both physically and mentally, think again!

So, when you are in denial about your true feelings, you are blocking your true feelings. The ancient Chinese art of acupuncture explains how blocking feelings causes a breakdown in our nervous system. In eastern medicine, the body is said to have many different channels or meridians. Blockage to any of these meridians causes energy to become restricted, instead of flowing freely into our bodies. It is a known fact, in the eastern culture and in parts of our western culture, that **NEGATIVE EMOTIONS DEPRESS THE IMMUNE SYSTEM.**

Positive thinking, on the other hand, allows energy to flow freely throughout our bodies. Meridians are not blocked and we stay healthy, both mentally and physically.

Three Steps to Breaking Denial

Just how do you distinguish between denial and positive thinking? How do you find out if there is still emotional pain that needs to be healed? And how do you break your denial?

There are three steps to breaking denial:

1. Journaling
2. Sharing your journal with a trusted friend
3. Hearing others tell their stories

Step 1: Journaling

Journaling is the act of writing out your experiences, and then writing about whatever feelings come up for you as you're recalling the experiences. If you never take your pen from the paper as you're journaling about these feelings, before long, whatever is in your heart will come out onto the paper. Journaling is healthy because it helps you take what's buried in your subconscious and get it out. It puts distance between you and the hurt and therefore, is a great emotional release. Also, if you're going to work through the hurts of your past, you must first remember why you hurt. You can't work through feelings until you face your hurts, and telling your story will also help break the denial. Remember, there's a thin line between denial and positive thinking. Breaking your denial will free you to think positively; it's one of your inner resources.

To illustrate how denial can operate in one's life, we'll go back to my own story. For years I denied that I was actually molested, because my perpetrator never touched me. But, when Mitchell forced me to masturbate him when I was an innocent little seven year old, probably a dozen different emotions flooded my being. I felt sickened inside; I felt fear, guilt, sadness and shame.

This one act triggered much in me; it literally changed the course of my life. To have my innocence destroyed in such a way was a real loss. As is the case with all young sexual abuse survivors, it robbed me of my childhood. For the rest of my young life, I was caught up in torment and agony. (I was one of the lucky ones; the devastation of a rape or incest survivor is much greater. But, this is not to diminish the demoralizing experience of my own reality.) When I was told that what had happened to me was in fact a molestation, my denial was broken. I was able to face the fact that I had been molested and could now work through the feelings. The denial I'd carried for years enabled me to minimize my experience. When this denial was finally broken, I was able to choose to think positively. It was that positive thinking that led me to the confrontation which healed my soul.

You Can't Work on your Issues
Unless you Break your Denial of Them!

In breaking your own denial about what happened to you in parochial school, it's helpful to write down your experiences. This is the first step. It's essential to recount the details, and to become aware of any feelings that come up for you. You have to first recognize the feelings in order to work through them.

Now, I'm not advocating anything I haven't already done myself. The way I got in touch with my feelings about my own adverse experiences in parochial school was to write it all down.

I went to a Catholic grade school from kindergarten through eighth grade. Being the first grandchild on my father's side of the family, I had always been showered with love and attention. I had a very happy home life with my parents. Upon entering kindergarten, I had my first taste of bitterness, harshness, and cruelty. It came in the shape of a little round nun in black and white. On the first day of kindergarten, I cried and cried. This particular nun called me "Cry Baby" and stood me in the corner for the entire day. I'd felt scared and wanted my mommy. Now, I felt shamed, embarrassed, and ostracized from the rest of the class. That was my first introduction to just how cruel the nuns could be.

I quickly became used to the nuns calling us names or yelling at us. Instead of separating the fact that we were precious children from the fact that we might be doing something that wasn't acceptable, they were covertly delivering sermons on how bad we were. There was always, in these sermons, an underlying current of shame—of somehow being defective and blemished—that ran through everything. In retrospect, my experience was that shame, guilt and fear were used as teaching tools and as a means to keep us under control at all times.

Mitchell had started molesting me when I was in second grade, and I was carrying a lot of unrealistic guilt from that. Between my guilt concerning the molestations and the guilt doled out by the nuns, I felt that no matter what I did, I was doomed to burn in Hell forever. I developed a very severe case of what is called scruples—thinking that everything I did was a sin.

This was around the same time that our class was preparing to make our First Confession and receive First Communion. We were guided through our "examination of conscience," which was a call to mind of all our sins so that we could later confess to the priest. At seven years of age, we were already well-versed on sin and the damnation of hellfire which was the penalty for committing mortal sins. (If you don't come from a Catholic background, mortal sins are grievous wrongs that, if done intentionally and if left untold in confession, are cause and provocation for going to Hell. Venial sins are smaller sins, not quite as grievous and don't zap you to Hell.)

So, there I was, preparing for my First Confession with another mean-spirited nun. This one, Sister Carmella, (not her real name) was our second grade teacher and she was one of the meanest women I've ever met. There was no emphasis on a loving Father in Heaven who loves little children and created them as innocent beings. Instead, Sister Mary Meany instilled in us a real fear of the confessional. She did this in her sermons on making a "bad confession" (leaving out a mortal sin), and by telling us scary stories. One such story was about a woman who purposely left mortal sins out of her confessions; one day, while the woman was in confession, a pair of white-gloved hands appeared and began choking her.

The other story was about demonic possession. Sister Mary Meany told us once that if we didn't go to Mass every Sunday, the earth would open up, and we would drop straight down to Hell. The devil would then take over our body. What a devastating story for six and seven-year-olds to hear! Back then, we didn't need horror films like *Psycho*; we had nuns!

When the day came to actually practice in the real confessional, Sister Carmella played the part of the priest. She lined us up and we each took our turn. She had explained that we'd hear the partition go up in the dark confessional. This would mean that the kid on the other side of the confessional was done telling his sins, and now it was our turn to confess. But, I had my ears plugged with my fingers so that I wouldn't hear the other kid's confession. (I was deathly afraid of the consequences. God was keeping score!) So, when she pulled up the partition on my side, I wasn't sure if I should start. I waited. She yelled, "Well, hurry up, stupid. What are you waiting for?" Needless to say, my first confessional experience was tainted with fear and guilt, and impacted by her demeaning, "Hurry up, stupid!"

From second through eighth grades, I would torment myself every first Thursday of the month, when it was mandatory that good little Catholic children go to Confession and then Communion the next day. The examinations of conscience were read in class by the nun. We would be seated at our desks, with our heads resting on the top of the desk, arms folded underneath. The nun would rattle off her list of sins, going from commandment to commandment. So scared was I about entering that confessional again that I would get a sinking feeling in the pit of my stomach, and feel as though I had to defecate.

I was confused about a lot of things. When a "bad thought" came into my head, I thought I had sinned. I tried to count everything I thought might be a sin, but I couldn't remember. So, I resorted to making a list of my sins. Once I wrote my list of sins on a card which had a picture of the Madonna and Child on it. As always, I took it in to confession with me. Afterwards, I was afraid to throw it away. We had learned about sacrilege, but I wasn't clear on it. All we were told was that it had to do with the desecration of something holy. (I don't believe we were old enough to absorb or to correctly contextualize half of what we were told.) So, I decided that I'd be committing a sacrilege if I threw away the holy card with the list of sins on it. I hid it in an old binder and put it in my closet. I lived in fear that my mother would find it, but I was afraid to throw it away. One day, my mother did spring cleaning and threw away the binder. I still remember the relief I had felt.

Then there would be long periods of time—maybe months—when I'd push the molestation totally out of my consciousness. Sooner or later, something would remind me of the molestation, and the all-too-familiar "doomed to Hell" fear would be back. Then I'd start confessing again what was done to me because I felt I had sinned. Of course, it hadn't even been a sin on my part because it was forced on me, but the guilt I felt was unbearable.

The whole confessional thing became a dreaded ordeal for me. Because of the constant comments from the nuns about making a bad confession and going to Hell because of it, I thought that during the time I didn't remember, all the confessions I'd made were "bad" confessions and sacrileges because I had withheld sins. This, in turn, made all the communions I'd made "bad" communions and sacrileges as well. Every time I went to confession, I'd confess not only the molestation, but try to remember everything I did wrong between the time I was seven until the present.

One Sunday after Mass, I convinced myself that a particle of the host had fallen onto my clothing. I agonized for hours in my bedroom, on my hands and knees, picking up every piece of lint I saw, for fear it was part of the host. I was tormented because I knew we weren't supposed to touch the host (in those days) but I also knew I couldn't leave it on the floor!

I developed bizarre rituals. My parents called them nervous habits, but all I knew was that I had to do certain things like roll my neck or sweep imaginary germs from the sky, or something horrible would happen to the people in my family. Today, I know this as part of an obsessive compulsive disorder. (We'll discuss obsessive compulsive disorder—OCD—in a later chapter.)

Shame-based environments such as the one I was exposed to are breeding grounds for OCD, if one is psychologically predisposed to this disorder. This is why, after leaving parochial school for a public high school some years later, all my "nervous habits" completely disappeared.

During third grade, I developed a fear of the dark and a fear of being alone in a different part of the house than anyone else in the family. I just knew that some ghost or evil spirit from the depths of Hell would come to get me, based on the nun's demonic possession story and others like it.

There seemed to be a "hush, hush" rule at my school, much like Barbara had expressed in Chapter Two. So I too, told no one. No one, that is, except a loving, wonderful priest named Father Matthew. (This IS his real name. I pay tribute to him here; the man was a saint!) Father Matthew was my brief salvation from a relentless plague. Once, during one of my super-long confessions, he actually raised the partition to talk to me. I was mortified! He said, "Dianne, you're building a thick forest around you." And he gave my problem a name. He said I had "a bad case of scruples." And Father Matthew started counseling me through the scruples. He was a beautiful man with a beautiful voice which shook the church rafters when he sang *Ave Maria*. He died about twenty-five years ago. He was truly one of the angels of my life because he helped me begin to see that I was being unrealistic in blaming myself for everything.

However, I was still doing the "confessional rag" at the time of my eighth grade graduation. Leaving parochial school meant throwing in the towel. I walked away from all the religious rituals that I couldn't handle. Furthermore, I turned my back on God. The obsessive compulsive disorder stopped.

I no longer had to deal with scruples because I no longer cared. This was truly the beginning of my spiritual death.

All throughout my parochial school years, I'd had no reprieve from guilt, fear, and shame. In the third and fifth grades, when we were lucky enough to get a lay teacher instead of a nun, one of the nuns from another grade would come in once a week for more guilt, shame and fear. Perhaps the nun who both scared and scarred me the most was my sixth grade nun Sister Mary Luke, my old buddy who I mentioned in Chapter One. My eighth grade nun was also the principal of the school. I saw her pulling boys' noses and twisting boys' ears, shaking kids and pulling their arms nearly out of their sockets, for things like talking in line or not knowing the correct answer. These were all examples of abuse of some nature—physical, emotional, spiritual. The message to me and any other kid who had been an observer was that we should have fear and shame for who we are. And that, in and of itself, was abusive.

It had been extremely beneficial to me to recount these painful events on paper. Yes, it hurt considerably, but I knew that the only way out of the pain was straight through it. So, I recommend to you that you recount your own story on paper. Buy yourself a journal and start slowly.

It may help if, before you journal, you turn to Appendix I at the back of the book to read through the questionnaire that I used for this research. One of the purposes of this questionnaire was to let the people who'd gone to religious school voice their experiences, whether good or bad. Because this book is intended to be a recovery journey, you may find it very therapeutic to fill out the questionnaire because completing it may help in your own healing. Consider it a sturdy foundation with which to start to build your fortress of inner resources for healing the past—and for forgiving it.

Step 2: Sharing Your Journal with a Trusted Friend

After you've poured your heart out onto paper, the act of reading what you've written out loud will serve to heal you further. You can read it out loud to the walls, your dog or cat, or a friend with whom you would trust your life, if you have such a person in your life. This, in addition to journaling, will help you release negativity further.

Another way in which to release this "stuff" is to just get a match and set fire to the pages you just wrote and read out loud. This is a bit ceremonious, but you'll be surprised at the release you'll feel while watching those pages turn to ashes. This really helps put closure on the past.

Step 3: Hearing Others Tell their Stories

You've heard the old saying, "Misery loves company"? Usually, this has a negative connotation attached to it. Actually, in conjunction with dealing with emotional pain, it's very healing to be able to share with others. When this happens, you begin to realize that you're not alone. The knowledge that others have gone through similar experiences will help break the isolation and loneliness which often characterizes a person who has gone through any juvenile trauma. Subsequently, realizing that you're not alone will make it easier to stop denying your reality to yourself.

Some of the testimonies triggered by the questionnaire are being used throughout this book. They were shared very candidly and with painstaking honesty. Throughout these life experiences, you'll see a lot of examples of abuse. We need to recognize these people as the courageous survivors they are and acknowledge them as having a tender humanity. This tender humanity was damaged through contacts with shame-based people, who themselves had undoubtedly suffered at the hands of their own perpetrators.

Joseph's Story:

> "Well, I hate to sound negative, but each nun I had eventually picked out a scapegoat from one of the kids in our class. I was so aware of it that I began to dread the first day of school at the end of every summer break. I was always afraid that this year, it would be me. One year it was a girl who our teacher called 'Large Bones' all year, because she thought that the girl 'weighed too much.' All the kids started to call her that and no one would play with her all year. Another year, it was a chubby boy who the nun always seemed to pick on. She always gave him a hard time. Calling him up to the front of the class, she would embarrass him by telling him he was too fat and that his shoes were always dirty. Her favorite way of belittling that boy was to tell him not to ever take off his shoes because there might be such an odor that it would close the school for the day. During the year, he never talked to anyone except once in a while. When he did, he'd hang his head so low that you were embarrassed to even ask him a question. Many times, as punishment for something he'd never done, he'd have to stand with the wastebasket over his head in front of the room. It was always his job to pass the wastebasket

after lunch period, because in those days, we ate a packed lunch in our classrooms."

Ben's story:

"During the years that I was an altar boy, I was raped repeatedly in the basement of the rectory by a priest. The priest would start by teaching me to box so that I could protect myself. The boxing would end in improper touching and advances by the priest. I never told anyone; I was too ashamed and afraid that no one would believe me."

The Case of Father Porter

About nineteen years ago, over eighty people came forward to testify against Father Porter of North Attleboro, Massachusetts, for raping and sodomizing them when they were children. One man told of how Father Porter had coerced him with "boxing lessons," which he described in the same way Ben did.

At other times Father Porter would carry out his sickness with these children in their own homes, with their parents in another room. It was then that he'd quietly have them masturbate him. He would make them promise not to tell anyone because "no one would believe you anyway." They talked of being drugged by this priest during the incidents which were carried on away from their home. He would make them eat a certain pie that had been laced with something or make them drink communion wine.

Unthawing Feelings

The people who shared their stories with me all related that they'd felt a sense of shame. The shame was about feeling as though they'd done something dirty. The shame had triggered fear that if they'd told someone, they would be considered at fault and would've been punished.

The sexual abuse survivors that I interviewed all had related to me that they'd felt a major sense of guilt. Some of them still wonder, as adults, what they'd done wrong that caused them to be sought out among other classmates as a target.

It's helpful for you to take a look at the actual results of the study that appears in Appendix II. This may help break the denial further. By doing so, you can break free from your personal chains of the past.

Perhaps it's hard for you to read the stories presented in this text. If the stories triggered memories that need healing, this is good news. This means you've begun the first step. No matter how devastatingly painful the memories and the hurt, you can now work on them.

To deny that you feel the pain is to sabotage your spiritual and emotional growth. With pain comes growth. Sadly, it's only when we confront the painful feelings engendered by the hurtful events in our life that we learn to deal with and overcome adversity. Many times in my life, I've looked upward and said, "Enough growth, already!"

Besides pain, you've probably also found strength in the stories shared candidly and fearlessly by people with whom you can relate. They're brothers and sisters in your struggles. There's strength involved in a shared trauma, and healing goes along with that strength.

The work of erasing the thin line between positive thinking and denial entails a lot of soul-searching. If you've been working with me, you've just come through three steps to help break your denial. Congratulate yourself for bravely meeting the challenge!

Things to Remember After Reading Chapter III:

- You've done nothing wrong.
- You were a child who trusted adults.
- Those adults fell short of your trust because they were flawed.
- You were born precious and innocent.
- Your innocence may have been taken from you. However, no one can take away your preciousness.
- You are still precious. You will always be precious.

Affirmation for Chapter III:

"I am precious and I have regard for my tender humanity."

Chapter IV

Awareness and Yearning as Resources for Healing

Chapter IV
Awareness and Yearning as Resources for Healing

Let's see what we have so far in your journey toward healing from the abuse that may have been done to you as a child at the hands of the priests and nuns who taught you in school.

In Chapters I and II, I've suggested that if you've already utilized techniques for healing your past wounds concerning your family of origin, but haven't addressed the issue of abuse in the religious school system that you attended as a child, you may have done only half the work. Neurolinguistic Programming has been introduced as a method for getting in touch with feelings, healing the feelings, and finally forgiving your transgressors. We've talked about forgiveness being the last step in securing happiness, serenity and peace of mind in your life.

In Chapter Three, we've explored the three steps that can help you to break the denial in your life. I've presented the questionnaire and results of the study (available in Appendices II and III) that I'd conducted among "adult children of religious schools" to give you further strength and insight. Reading the study and subsequent stories help to break the denial.

AWARENESS AS A RESOURCE FOR HEALING

By now, you may be beginning to feel empowered in knowing that you aren't alone in your struggles to overcome residue from a hurtful past. You must, however, go through many steps to move from awareness to forgiveness. Becoming aware means you may have to focus your attention on some pretty raw parts of your heart.

Part of becoming aware is identifying the types of abuse you're dealing with. It helps to identify the hurt. When we give the demons that plague us a name, they lose their power. Awareness also leads to understanding, which leads to healing.

The abuses that are most prevalent in our society are physical abuse, sexual abuse, intellectual abuse, emotional abuse, and spiritual abuse.

Physical Abuse

We all know what physical abuse is. Physical abuse certainly was prevalent in the classroom of religious schools from the 1940's through the 1960's, when the "spare the rod and spoil the child" mentality was evident.

Kenneth's Story:

> "I lived in fear every day of the school year at my parochial school. I was so scared of getting smacked on the knuckles with a ruler, the way I saw the nuns do to other kids. Y'know, I still hear jokes today about nuns hitting kids with rulers and everyone laughs but me. It's not funny. Actually, it's part of a nightmare I'd just as soon forget."

"In sixth grade, something snapped. I became a hard guy in school. I think I was so sick of seeing my buddies get smacked with rulers, having their hair pulled, or getting punched in the arm, that I wanted to make something of it. I think my braveness was due to the sudden growth spurt I experienced. It seemed like it happened overnight. My height shot up and suddenly I was taller than all the nuns. I started mouthing off to my nun that year. She knew better than to mess with me, since I was now a whole head taller than she was. So, she called in her thug, Father Bob."

"Father Bob started showing up at recess time, or he would hang around the hallways. One day in class, my friend Karl was called to the blackboard to solve a math problem. He was having trouble so Sister started brow-beating him. He was all red in the face, trying to come up with the right answer. Sister was getting very impatient with him. She had hold of the back of his neck, and she began applying pressure. Every time he guessed wrong about part of the algebra procedure we were learning, she pressed harder with her hand around the back of his neck."

"I couldn't take this anymore. My friend was being humiliated and I could see that he was in physical pain. I guess all the years of keeping back my fear is what motivated me, because the next thing I knew, I was out of control. I guess I really snapped! I flew up to the front of the class and pushed Sister back, so that she would stop hurting my buddy. Well, the next thing I knew, the classroom door was flung open and in ran Father Bob. He must've been lurking around in the hallway and heard all the noise. I'm sure I heard a kid or two scream. He ran right up to the front of the classroom and knocked me into the wall. He didn't go any further than that; I suppose the man had a lot of self-control. The lunch bell rang just then and everyone seemed to calm down. I was taken to the principal's office. They called my parents and had me expelled from school. My father went down to the priest's rectory and talked to him. Knowing my dad, I think he probably talked rather loudly. Anyway, at least I was able to get out of there. I was enrolled in a public school the next week."

Besides the blatant act of physically harming a child, there are other methods of abusing a child physically. If there is a lack of physical nurturing at home, for example, this is a more covert form of physical abuse. It's sad to say, but we live in a society which must leave physical nurturing out of the classroom for fear that it may be misconstrued as sexual molestation.

SEXUAL ABUSE

Jonathan's Story:

"I was sexually abused by a priest in the sacristy of a Catholic Church when I was in sixth grade. It happened twice. [The sacristy is the area adjacent to the altar, where the priests and altar boys get ready for the Mass.] On both occasions, when everyone had left after Mass, he gave me some leftover communion wine. The priest said it wasn't a sin because he, a priest, was giving it to me to cleanse my soul. It was a way of getting closer to God, he had told me the first time. When I started to feel dizzy from the wine, he sodomized me. When I look back on all that, it really sickens me and makes me angry."

Jonathan's story sickens me and makes me angry, too. Molestation is an obvious form of sexual abuse, as are rape and incest. But what about subtler forms that sometimes go unnoticed? A female participant of my study told me that when she was fourteen and fully developed, her grandfather, who lived in their house, would open the bathroom door (which didn't have a lock) when he knew she was in there. As she stood half-naked to wash herself, he'd yell at her that she was taking too long. This happened twice that she can recall. After the first time, it certainly couldn't be called a mistake. He knew what he'd see. This act was not only abusive because it transgressed her boundaries, but his yelling helped to attach a negative feeling (shame) to her body.

When fathers make references to their daughters' bodies with sexual innuendos, such as "you're getting big boobies like your mamma" or when mothers tell their sons that they "hope you'll have a big pee-pee like your daddy's," this is extreme sexual abuse, no matter what the tone of voice in which it is delivered.

Part of my own history, which I shared with you in the last chapter, had to do with my sixth grade teacher, the nun who sexually molested Jeremy. Even when she made references like "very soon you'll know the reason that I separated the boys' rows from the girls' rows," it was an invasion of sexual boundaries, and therefore sexually abusive.

In that small mid-western town in the late 1950's, we were very sheltered. Most of us did not know about sex yet. As hard as it may be to believe today, when children can be exposed to explicit sex on cable TV and the internet every day, many of we girls were just learning about having our periods back then, while the boys were just learning how and why their penises got erect in the middle of the night. It was an innocent time. And when holy innocence is stolen from a child, it's like adding ammonia to a bouquet of beautiful lilacs.

Intellectual Abuse

Many classroom cases of intellectual abuse came out of the study. When an adult infers that a child's thinking is wrong because the adult's is right, that is intellectual abuse. Everyone has a right to think on their own, but intellectual abuse shatters your way of thinking. It says, in effect, "You can't even think right. You have a defective brain." When children are told repeatedly that they are defective, they begin to believe it. Elaine's story is indicative of this type of abuse.

Elaine's Story:

> "I went to an all-girls' parochial school from grades nine through twelve. Those four years were a nightmare. I'd always gone to a public elementary school and loved it. I'd never experienced any name-calling by the teachers, until ninth grade. We had nuns and priests who taught us. One priest called me a 'lamebrain' or a 'nitwit' whenever he referred to me. When he called on me to answer a question, he'd say things like, 'I doubt that you'll know, but try anyway.' Once he looked right at me as he said, 'Lots of people never make it in life. They go around always wishing they had things but aren't smart enough to get them.' He emphasized 'smart enough' and raised his eyebrows at me. A few of the other girls laughed at this. I was so ashamed and embarrassed! When it was time for us to choose our college classes in twelfth grade, he made all my choices for me. Everyone else was able to decide what they wanted to be. He told me I was probably going to need help and that he'd help me. He said I'd probably end up marrying the first guy who'd have me. He was extremely abusive toward me. I also saw other kids get abused by him."

Being called "stupid," "nitwit," and "lamebrain" constitutes intellectual abuse. Another example of intellectual abuse committed against a child would be an adult who makes all the child's choices for him. The inference is that the child cannot think for himself. When over-protective parents or teachers do this, they are helping to produce people who have difficulty making decisions and choices on their own all their lives.

Emotional Abuse

Arthur's tale is a good example of emotional abuse, which is very closely related to intellectual abuse.

Arthur's Story:

> "I was having a happy life in a nice public school. Then, one Sunday in church, the pastor told all the parents that if their kids were in a public school, they were 'under pain of mortal sin' and would go to hell!"

> "This guilt trip worked on my parents, because the following Monday, I found myself wearing navy blue uniform pants and a light blue uniform shirt, smack in the middle of a Catholic school. I hated leaving my friends, but what was really nasty was the way the nuns yelled and screamed and badgered the boys. They seemed to leave the girls alone. Maybe they felt that it built character in the boys and that they could take it. I was smacked on the arm or hand a time or two, but it was nothing I couldn't handle. It still really annoys me though, the way that priest used guilt and shame to control my parents, my life and my sister's life. Sure he wanted us in his school; think of the tuition! As a kid, I never questioned his integrity as a priest. Many years later, I heard that he had had a mistress for a long time."

Arthur's priest had used guilt as a ploy to manipulate and control Arthur's parents and every other parent in the church that day. The objective may or may not have been to raise church revenue by receiving tuition by more church members. It may have been a genuine concern on the priest's part to "save souls." Regardless of the objective, adults and children were being exploited through guilt.

Chapter IV. Awareness and Yearning as Resources for Healing

The adult children of religious schools who told of being called "tubby" and "cry baby" or who were told they were a "wimp" for crying when their dog died, were also being abused emotionally.

Another form of emotional abuse is a parent or teacher constantly screaming at a child (or a classroom of kids) because that parent or teacher doesn't know how to discipline in a healthy way. Emotional abuse can be a parent or teacher ridiculing a child's fear of the dark, or anything else that the child fears. A parent neglecting to nurture the child with "I love you" or being otherwise emotionally unavailable is another example of emotional abuse.

Spiritual Abuse

In the religious school system, spiritual abuse is the strongest area of abuse. The list of grievances in this area is endless and lends itself easily to the religious school system, by its very nature. Spiritual abuse is demanding perfection from children or being over-controlling. It's giving a sense that God is a punitive God, who demands perfection and is waiting to zap us to Hell or send a horrible malady our way for any sin that we commit.

Another form of spiritual abuse presents itself when children are given conflicting messages about God, which is depicted on the cover of this book.

Rebecca's Story:

> "Overall, the nuns and priests instilled a real fear of God in me. They really turned me off toward Him; made me feel He was mean. From the very start, I remember being told that God was someone to fear; someone who was always waiting to punish. The first week of Kindergarten, I cried every day because I wanted my mother. The nun called me a little brat and told me, 'Don't you know your mother won't come for you if you keep crying?'"

> "And in fifth grade, another nun pulled me out of line in church and smacked me across the face so hard that I actually

fell into two other kids! I didn't even know why. Later, I found out it was because I had forgotten my hat twice in a row, and I only had a hanky on my head. Do you remember how the girls had to wear something on their heads in church? Anyway, she told me that I was offending God and really made me feel like the worst possible sinner in the world."

"I remember all that vividly. My mother, who saves everything, still has a picture that I made in school. The picture was done on red construction paper. My mother says I brought it home the first day of second grade. In crayon, I had drawn a big black circle with legs. In the circle, it said *COD*. (I had meant *God*.) Next to 'COD,' I had drawn my teacher. She was a nun so it was easy to scribble a long black veil and long black dress. The nun and the black circle 'COD' had a big green stick and they were hitting a little girl. It was me. I'd drawn myself. There was a big arrow pointing from myself to where I had spelled my name, in very tiny letters in the corner. That picture still haunts me. What I mean is, whenever my mother drags out all the dusty old memorabilia from my school days and I look at that picture, I get the weirdest sensation. Then, I feel really gloomy all day and can't seem to kick it."

Spiritual abuse comes, too, when children are given a negative sense of self. This will lead to difficulty believing that they're loveable to God, to anyone, or to themselves.

Betty's Story:

"Because of the way the nuns carried on, I remember thinking that it was a mortal sin to even like a boy. But how could I deny what was in my heart? One day, I was caught passing a note about a boy to my girlfriend. The next day, I got a severe talking to about liking boys. And I got punished. I had to write three hundred times that I was going to go to hell if I didn't stop liking Martin. Then, I had to read it in front of the whole class. I was so embarrassed; and so was Martin! She actually made me stand up there and read it! Oh, she stopped me after several agonizing minutes. By that time, I was very red in the face and I could feel my cheeks becoming hotter and hotter. That was among my worst memories."

Chapter IV. Awareness and Yearning as Resources for Healing

The nun in Betty's story gave the message to Betty that she was somehow a bad person for developing an infatuation and should be ashamed of the natural process of growing up. Since Betty could do nothing to shut off that human response to puberty, she was made to feel unhealthy shame and that she was defective as a person. This is an example of spiritual abuse.

Furthermore, when teachers or parents carry a "better than" attitude, such attitudes are interpreted by their children adversely. The message destroys the very core of spirituality for them. True spirituality has respect for every person's tender humanity. Grandiosity carries the "more than, less than" mentality which breeds codependent attitudes.

Some parents and teachers don't give any information about true spirituality. Rather, they concentrate on being "religious" and not committing "mortal sin," as if any one sin is a greater separation from God than the other. Actually, an atheist can be more spiritual than a person who prides himself on being highly religious. Spirituality is about a high regard for tender humanity, both our own and everyone else's. (I know of some "highly religious" people who actually have crushed their own and other's spirituality in the name of religion.)

Parents and teachers who abandon children emotionally make it hard for the child to conceive of a God always being there for them. This attitude, as well as the others mentioned, can be carried into adulthood. Emotional abandonment is about being physically present but emotionally distant. This is also spiritually abusive.

It is spiritual abuse whenever parents or teachers are judgmental, blaming, rejecting, or non-affirming to children. Moreover, whenever parents or teachers use the concept of God to frighten or control their children, these are also examples of spiritual abuse.

Yearning as a Resource for Healing

Now that we've named some of the demons, let's take a second to catch our breaths. Perhaps the stories you've just read were disturbing to some of you, particularly to those who are just getting in touch with these dysfunctional behaviors as they operated in your childhood. Take a few deep breaths. Breathe in through your nose, hold for the count of three, and now let that breath flow out your mouth. Breathe again. Say to yourself, "I'm a loveable and worthwhile person." This is to replace the negativity that you may have thought about while reading the descriptions of the different types of abuse.

I realize this may be very intense material for some of you. Therefore, take it slowly. Be gentle and kind to yourself. Remember that the only way out of the pain is through it. Remember to breathe. As you read, you may want to keep affirming to yourself that you're a loveable, worthwhile person. Say out loud, "I'm a loveable, worthwhile person." This is an auditory way in which to affirm your self esteem. Now, put down the book and give yourself a hug. That's right. Wrap your right arm around your left shoulder and your left arm around your right shoulder. Now, squeeze gently. This affirms your self esteem kinesthetically. Repeat your affirmation. "I'm a loveable, worthwhile person." Now, stand in front of your mirror and repeat your hug as you tell yourself, "I am a loveable, worthwhile person." You've just solidified to yourself visually that you're a loveable and worthwhile person.

You may not feel loveable and worthwhile yet. But, if you have a desire in your heart to feel that you're loveable and worthwhile, you'll begin to feel it. Go ahead—yearn for that feeling of being loveable and worthwhile. You *will* get there. The more you yearn for something, the easier it becomes to attain. When you want something so bad you can taste it, this is a yearning of your heart. And when that happens, whatever it is for which you yearn will come to pass. I know from personal experience.

As I've said, I'd turned away from God after my "extreme case of scruples" as a child. After eighth grade graduation in 1961, I turned my back and buried my pain. I couldn't cope with the pressure I felt from believing everything I did was a mortal sin. I didn't know how to separate God from the difficult way in which I was taught to worship Him. The God of my youth was a punitive God. Obviously, I didn't know the real God then.

Let me jump way ahead to September 1983. I had spent over twenty years trying to stuff down the pain of the molestation and the shame, fear, guilt and pain that I felt, with food and men. These were my drugs. I was the original Queen of Relationship Addiction; bouncing from one relationship to another; marrying three times. My weight went up and down, depending on whether or not I wanted a man in my life.

My son Ron and my daughter Marianna and I lived in the midwest. I was busy setting up a small business, when I began experiencing sporadic neurological symptoms. Essentially, the muscles from my neck up failed to work a lot of the time. I couldn't swallow, my voice would get inaudible, and I could not wink my eyes. During a bout with pneumonia, the symptoms were intensified. After the pneumonia was gone, the symptoms were even more intense. I couldn't even swallow water or baby food! My own saliva made me choke; my voice was now very weak and faint. I struggled to be understood. Since the blinking reflex in my eyes was very slow, my eyes always felt as though they were taped open. My tongue felt awkward in my mouth, as though it was ten times its natural size. The entire sensation felt as though I was being buried alive!

During this time, when I felt abandoned and afraid, I received a package in the mail. My parents had just returned from Lourdes and the Holy Land, and my mother had sent me some souvenirs, among them a bottle of holy water from Lourdes. I remember drinking some, saying to a friend that "if this doesn't cure me, nothing will." In essence, I was praying to God without really praying. It was an indirect plea for help, because in those days I didn't believe that God wanted to hear from me.

Shortly after that, I decided to move back to Phoenix and a warmer climate. I knew something was wrong neurologically and that I couldn't risk any more bouts with pneumonia, which might trigger other crises.

Well, God had heard my indirect prayer to Him. Shortly after moving to Phoenix, through a series of "chance happenings," I was led to Beginning Experience, the divorce recovery program I mentioned earlier. (B.E. is open to all faiths and is conducted through the Roman Catholic Church. Funny how Catholicism was and still is an influence in my life, though now I refer to myself as a non-denominational Christian.)

When I entered the chapel for that Rite of Reconciliation during that November 1984 B.E. weekend I talked about earlier, I had been away from God for twenty-three years. After the service in which I was able to forgive those nuns and priests from my childhood, we were invited to go talk to a priest. I found myself talking to a priest who was on the B.E. team. I told him that I wasn't ready to come back to God yet, but I knew that something very real had moved me. By the next morning at breakfast, I told the priest that I'd let God back into my life. He smiled, hugged me and welcomed me back. He said, "I knew you would." I still remember the renewed peace and serenity I had felt that day.

The thing that has touched me the most about God in these many years of our friendship is that He never gave up on me. Even when I wanted nothing to do with Him, He stayed with me. He got me to my first B. E. weekend by using people in my life; that's how He works.

You see, He knew something I didn't know yet. He knew that I was already in the beginning stages of a debilitating disease called Myasthenia Gravis. He knew that I would need Him in my life for strength; that all the muscles from my neck up would periodically fail to work effectively. He knew that I would need Him for strength so that I could proclaim that Myasthenia Gravis may weaken my body but could never weaken my inner strength and spirit. He was that strength for me and I know that if I hadn't had God in my life, I could never have survived and conquered this challenge.

I became a member of the B.E. team shortly after that 1984 weekend. My condition at that time still remained undiagnosed. In the next two years, my illness progressed to the point that, in order to give my presentations on B. E. weekends, I had to use a tape recorder (remember those things?) and take up to two weeks to tape a seven minute presentation. This was because my throat muscles didn't work properly. Therefore, the only way I could be understood when I talked was to say a few words into the recorder each morning while I still had some muscle strength. Instead of making the presentation to the group of participants, we would have to play my tape for them.

Although the symptoms were with me constantly, I was yet undiagnosed. On one B.E. weekend, a participant who didn't know my circumstances tried to speak to me at mealtime. In those days, it was almost impossible for me to talk while eating since the same muscles are involved for both tasks. This makes the muscles tire more rapidly, often causing choking to occur. I had tried to answer her and had started to choke. After someone had assisted me in dislodging the food, I stepped into the chapel and cried out to God, "Please help me to be like everyone else. I want to be able to eat without choking. Help me!"

And God answered me. My doctor says I'm a walking miracle. I am! God gave me a second chance! Now I use my strong voice to lecture at colleges and in classrooms; I lead LifeDance Therapy Workshops, and record self-hypnosis compact discs. God has really given me a second chance!

Of course, he didn't just zap me well. There were lessons to be learned; the blessings of my illness. He led my brother John to my door one night to tell me of a good neurologist who was to correctly diagnose my condition when others had failed. But before that diagnosis, God gave me the necessary knowledge I needed to aide in my own recovery.

While still an undergraduate, I learned of guided imagery being taught to cancer patients. Patients are told to visualize the cancer cells being eaten up by healthy cells. When I was diagnosed, I read all I could about MG to find out exactly what was happening in my body that created my symptoms.

With this new-found knowledge, I went to a friend who teaches psychology at a local junior college. I asked him to actually draw me a picture (since I'm a visual person) of the brain and what happens to the muscles of healthy bodies in terms of muscle reflex, nerve impulses and neurotransmitters.

After he drew the images, I could get a clear picture of things. It really put things into perspective for me. Then I made an audio tape (well, it *was* 1986) of my feeble voice affirming that what wasn't yet happening in my body was actually happening. For example, the tape was full of statements like, "the muscles in my neck are healthy, strong, and relaxed."

I played that tape at least twice a day. When I heard my feeble voice, I actually yearned to be well, so much that I could taste it. I felt the yearning in my heart! (To go back to our chapter on NLP strategies, my strategy for getting well, then, was visual-to-auditory-to-kinesthetic because I first needed to see a picture of the situation, and then make an audio tape to listen to, which brought on the kinesthetic state of yearning.)

Today I'm healthy and strong. My MG returns occasionally, but not as severely as it used to. And when it does, it's because I'm under a tremendous amount of stress. In that case it may cause double vision and loss of voice volume. That's my warning to slow down my life.

Through lots of prayers from many people and through positive thinking, affirmations, visualization, and using my God-given intellect, I am a walking, talking miracle!

I relate all of this to you as an illustration of what the power of the mind can do. Yearning; wanting something so badly you can taste it. I think that yearning reconciles the soul.

Chapter IV. Awareness and Yearning as Resources for Healing

When we feel hardened and embittered by someone's abuse toward us, we have the ability to overcome those feelings. All we have to do is want it badly enough, and God will give us the strength to do it.

So yearn! And feel your yearnings. Use that yearning of your heart as a resource for healing. It's already there. Feel it. Use it. One of the blessings of my illness is regard and respect for my tender humanity, and the tender humanity of each one of you. God never gives up on us, so we must be very special!

Things to Remember After Reading Chapter IV:

- You have a right to heal.
- You deserve to be happy.
- You are a good person.
- None of this was your fault.
- You have a right to desire that good things happen to you.
- Good things DO happen to you.

Affirmation for Chapter IV:

"I deserve to be happy!"

Chapter V

Understanding as a Resource for Healing

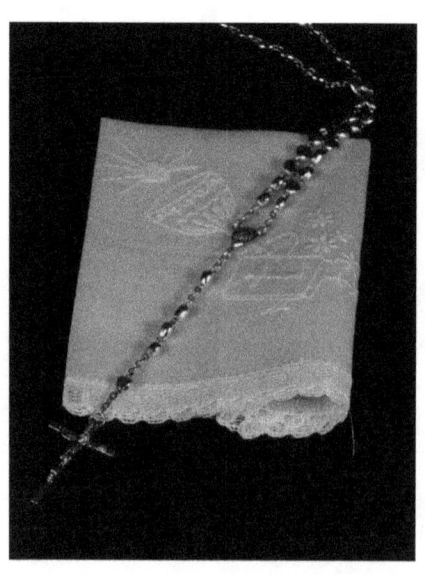

Chapter V
Understanding as a Resource for Healing

SONETTA TRISTE

(Sad Sonnet)

Melancholy moods give way to disdain;

Placid sensations explode with remorse;

Elusive patterns form from silent rain that

blocks the sun and that black clouds endorse.

Retrospect seems merely redundant or

is this what they mean by obsessive thought?

Sad reverie in abundance or

is this self-punishment which I have sought?

"Now the answer lies inward," a voice

speaks from deep within my soul.

"Power is there to take, it is your choice.

Serenity and hope help play the role."

Morose ponderings still plague and I implore

and yet, I won't play victim anymore!

Gloomy stuff, isn't it? As bleak as this little poem may be, let's just get a good laugh at the absurdity of the dismal first two stanzas. Observed in the written word, it shows the melodramatic plight of a person who is really entrenched in their victim role!

I wrote that silly poem in freshman year of high school for an assignment, which had been to write a very sad sonnet. I remember how I struggled with it for days, because that period of my life had been a particularly happy time. Now, many years later, this sonnet serves to set the stage for the heavy-duty discussion in which we are about to embark.

A large part of this chapter is devoted to a discussion about the moods and mindsets of the four different personality types, also called temperaments. We will also look at the three *preferred sensory modes*—visual, auditory and kinesthetic. We will explore the psychological condition known as Obsessive-Compulsive Disorder (OCD). The discussion about temperaments, preferred sensory modes, and the introduction to OCD, is necessary to help you to have a greater understanding (as the title of this chapter suggests), of what may have contributed to your grief in the first place.

Through my study among adult children of religious schools, I've found that when a person has a temperament known as *Melancholy*, and/or prefers the *Kinesthetic* sensory mode, the result may be a more vulnerable nature. In their childhood, (and later as an adult), such a person may be more susceptible to internalizing abuse directed at them than are other children. Also, a child possessing these components can be much more susceptible to becoming recipients of abusive behavior than others. We'll take a look at the second part of my study and find out what percentage of adult children who felt they'd been severely abused in the parochial school system, were actually Melancholy/Kinesthetic.

And, we'll establish why people respond differently to abuse. Understanding how we deal with abuse based on our personality and our leading sensory mode is important. Without blaming ourselves in the process, it will help us take responsibility for how and why it's so hard to get past the hurt we still carry.

In our talk about OCD, we'll find out how it can contribute to vulnerabilities, and can contribute to a person's internalization of abuse or what they perceive as abuse. We'll then deal with how shame operated as a part of the founding system of religious schools, especially in the 1940's through the 1960's. We'll discuss the motivating force that can attract abusive, shame-based people to the ministries to become a nun or a priest, or to enter the teaching profession.

But first, we need to have a discussion about what happened to the Catholic Church after all the changes took place in the 1960s as a result of the Vatican II conference. This will lay the groundwork for the rest of this chapter.

Dealing with Abandonment: Why Did They Change all the Rules?

The process of worshipping God was divinely intended to be very simple. Isn't it sad to note that we invest needless energy trying to measure up to various man-made dogma? Each religious denomination has its own set of rules. Catholics will remember the "Don't eat meat on Friday" rule as well as the "Go to confession every First Friday of the month" rule and the "Women must wear hats on their heads in church" rule. Many fundamentalists cannot dance or wear makeup. Do *this* a certain way. Do *that* a certain way. People get caught up in organized religion and somehow God gets lost in the shuffle. God gets lost along the way to the "perfect religious life." All God says is know Him and respect everyone's tender humanity. God really doesn't care about a lot of the things that hang us up.

It is a tragedy that a lot of people have turned away from God for many years because they gave up. They gave up trying to measure up. Somehow along the way they got the misinformation, whether it was conveyed overtly or covertly, that God was some tyrannical boogie man sitting up in Heaven, counting all the bad things, ready to zap people to Hell because of their sins. Love didn't enter into it at all; only hellfire, brimstone, and the gnashing of teeth, whatever that is. In their fear they never heard God say, "But I never meant it to be that difficult."

The *McGraw-Hill Catholic Encyclopedia* (1967) tells us that in January of 1957, three months after his election, Pope John XXIII assembled seventeen cardinals in the Abbey of St. Paul to review the religious situation of Rome. It was his hope that a "new Pentecost" would emerge from this. The same Catholic Encyclopedia goes on to say that the leaders of the church were striving to "make doctrine more understandable, constitution more simple and directives for safeguarding and developing morality more clear." They hoped for a "striking manifestation of the church's unity."

A great change took place in the Catholic Church in the 1960's after that ecumenical council known as Vatican II. This transformation, while done to unify Christians of all faiths, left many Catholics feeling betrayed and embittered. It seemed to them that many of the principles with which they shaped their lives were no longer valid.

This segment of the chapter deals with the results of changing some of the rules and how that may have triggered abandonment issues in some people who grew up in dysfunctional homes. (Abandonment issues here refer to what makes a person feel deserted and lonely.)

Here are just a few rules that were changed:

1. Women no longer have to cover their heads in church.

2. People wishing to receive communion in the morning no longer have to fast from midnight.

3. The Mass is no longer in Latin.

4. It is no longer a sin to eat meat on Friday.

5. The Mass was changed so that after the Lord's Prayer is recited, the people exchange the sign of Peace with a handshake.

6. During communion, the host can now be taken by hand, instead of the priest having to place it on the communicant's tongue. Also, the congregation is now offered the chalice of wine, if they desire.

Feedback from Catholics Concerning the Changes

There was nothing formal on the questionnaire that I circulated for several years, concerning the issue of the repercussions, if any, of the rules changing. However, while speaking at several Catholic churches in the southern suburbs of Detroit from 1992-1995, I took a small sampling among Catholics between the ages of sixty to sixty-five. This was completely independent of the study reflected herein. Most of these two hundred-eighty people had not attended a Catholic school in their youth.

Completely independent of the subject matter for those speaking engagements, and as research for this book, these people were asked to recall how they felt when some thirty years prior, their church changed some of the rules. Here is some of the feedback I got:

"They were not all rapid changes. I don't recall any adverse effects. I just went with it."

"I felt a real freedom. I always felt sick to my stomach, having to fast from midnight."

"When the changes came I started going to Communion more often."

"I don't do well with change. It took me a longtime to actually like the Mass said in English."

"My wife and I still don't eat meat on Friday. That is what the tradition was for many years."

Some Catholics Lost Trust in the Church

When a lot of the major rules were changed, many people felt like the rug had been pulled out from under them. The Catholic Church lost a lot of credibility with some of its faithful followers. For instance, for years Catholics were taught that the pope, when it comes to religious doctrine, is infallible. If the pope were predicting the weather, he could make a mistake. But, when it comes to dogma, no mistakes were ever made. It was that simple. Weather = mistakes, dogma = no mistakes, ever! Well, when a lot of the more popular saints were de-canonized after the Vatican Council, a lot of long-time Catholics couldn't deny that some pope, somewhere down the line, had made a mistake. Now, was it the pope who canonized St. Christopher? Or was it the pope who kicked him out?

Feelings of Abandonment Reported

Over the last twelve years as a psychotherapist, I've recognized a trend in my patients and clients who had been devout Catholics either before or during the time the Church changed all the rules. Many times during heavy-duty trauma work, present-day abandonment issues were traced, not only to their family of origin, but to the feeling they had of being forsaken or deserted by their church.

People Resist Change

When the great Catholic metamorphosis came, there were many people who quit going to church. They "fell away" from the Catholic Church and "fell away" from God as well. For many, the Catholic Church and God were synonymous.

Many people take issue with change in general. Some Catholics were delighted with the changes. The late comedian George Carlin used to do a whole comic routine many years ago about all the changes in the Catholic Church. I loved the way he joked about the old "no meat on Friday" rule. He said, "It's no longer a sin but I'll bet there are still people in Hell doing time on a meat rap!"

Chapter V. Understanding as a Resource for Healing

In addition to feedback on this matter from several groups of active senior-aged Catholics, I took the opportunity to pose the question about the Catholic church changing the rules to several groups of Adult Children of Alcoholics whom I had been addressing from 1992-1996. There was no specific age group here and the speaking engagements were held in California, Michigan and Canada.

Whether these people were Californians, mid-westerners or French Canadians, there was a common thread of discontent that weaved throughout our discussions. The commonality was that they had lived in a dysfunctional home as a child, where one or both their parents were alcoholic. If a person came from a dysfunctional family where one or both parents were emotionally unavailable due to, but not limited to, alcoholism, workaholism, or drug addiction, they grew up feeling alone and abandoned. The core issue with these people was a real feeling of abandonment which was magnified when their church changed the rules.

Or perhaps other issues inherent in adult children of dysfunctional backgrounds surfaced with the changes. For instance, many Catholics took for granted the part of the Mass where people offer each other the sign of peace. Some people welcomed this Vatican II change, while others viewed it as a real invasion of boundaries to have to interact with people with a handshake.

If you fall into the category of people with the type of dysfunctional family background I've just described, I would advise you to seek professional help with some inner child work, in conjunction with these exercises.

The main thing to remember is that you are just as precious now as the moment of your birth! When you feel abandoned, be fully present for yourself. You do this by being true to yourself. This means follow your heart and don't compromise your values. When you are honest with yourself, you have integrity. When you act with integrity, you are present for yourself.

Changes Meant Freedom to Many

In 1998, I interviewed Diane Geller, who is from a Catholic parish in Phoenix, Arizona. Diane instructs and prepares people who wish to embrace the beliefs of Catholicism and be baptized into that faith. I needed to get clear on what is still being taught as dogma and what is not. A lot of you ex-Catholics may be surprised to know that the old mortal sin/venial sin thing is no longer a focus. Nor is there a Limbo anymore, where all the babies and people who died before they got baptized would go. As George Carlin used to say, "I hear they did away with Limbo. Gee, I hope they didn't just cut people loose into space somewhere."

Purgatory used to be where you'd go if you died without mortal sin, only venial sins. (Now, it's also a place in Colorado to go skiing.) The idea was to stay there until you burned off all the venial sins and then you could go to Heaven. Ms. Geller, who is a convert from the Jewish faith, was surprised when I told her about the way the old indulgences could be earned by praying for a person who had died so that, if their soul was in Purgatory, they could get out sooner. A lot of the old catechisms and prayer books would include the exact number of days the person's stay in Purgatory would be shortened if you said that prayer for them. Some of the prayers, when done in a certain amount of reps, could even mean a complete release from Purgatory. Diane laughed and said, "It sounds like the souls in Purgatory could rack up flyer points and bonus miles like the airlines."

And that entire confession drama that used to traumatize children is now perceived very differently. It is no longer necessary to go to confession. The old rationale of doing so before communion was that if you went to communion with a mortal sin on your soul, you would be committing a sacrilege, which was worse than just an ordinary mortal sin. But, isn't the point of communion to commune with our Maker? And, aren't we all sinners?

The present Catholic dogma is no longer a condemnation doctrine. They emphasize a personal relationship with God.

Confession is now encouraged only because it is good for the soul. We've all confided in a friend from time to time to lift a burden. The sense of freedom is tremendous.

Knowledge of Personality Type Can Help Heal!

Let's shift our energy a bit and talk about the four temperaments, because your temperament is a major factor in how you react to what could be perceived as abandonment. The four temperaments (or personality types) go all the way back to Hippocrates around 400 B.C. The four temperaments are Sanguine, Choleric, Melancholy, and Phlegmatic. Knowing what temperament you are is just as important as knowing with what sensory system you lead.

With that in mind, I will encapsulate for you the highlights of each personality temperament:

Sanguines love people and love to be with them. Upon walking into a party, look at the colorful person who is the center of attention, with many people clustered around him or her. This is a Sanguine. They're the "life of the party" type, always telling stories and embellishing every detail. They're always outgoing, with bubbly personalities. Sanguines are optimistic and always have the most fun. People are drawn to them instantaneously. They have charisma, so they make friends easily. Mr. Webster describes the word *sanguine* as ... "full of blood; of the color of blood; cheerful; confident."

Cholerics are convincing, energetic, motivating, forceful and powerful. They're outgoing and optimistic in their approach to life. Show me a person who always wants to be in charge and is resourceful, and I'll show you a Choleric. They're born leaders who get more done than the other temperaments. They're very goal oriented, with a will of iron. They have a "take charge" attitude and are very domineering. The word *choleric* means "easily angered."

Phlegmatic people are stable and balanced. They aren't impressed easily. They just like to keep an even keel all throughout their lives. They don't take themselves or life too seriously. Overall, they're peaceful and easy to get along with. Nothing seems to bother Phlegmatics; they're content watching others busy themselves with their own lives. Phlegmatics are very flexible and adaptable with a pleasant disposition. Because of their balanced nature, they will neither be sublime nor ridiculous. They are so peace-loving that they'll go to great lengths to avoid conflict and do the same to avoid decision making. Unlike Sanguines, they never like to be in the spotlight. They're never pushy or domineering; this would indeed go against their grain. You can count on Phlegmatics to be forever calm and logical; loyal and patient. They're never impulsive and can be relied upon in a crisis to stay calm. Phlegmatics accept people as they are. The definition of *phlegmatic* is "cool and collected; unemotional."

Those are three of the four temperaments. For our purposes here, we're going to be discussing the melancholy temperament more in-depth.

Melancholy Temperament

Now that you have a basis of comparison, you'll get more out of our discussion on Melancholies.

Melancholies are very introspective, talented and creative people. They follow through with things, especially if they can see the long-range value. They are very orderly, neat and have set very high standards for themselves. They have a deep concern and compassion for others.

The definition of melancholy is "depression of spirits; morbidity; gloomy; depressed; pensive." And, interestingly enough, in an old 1978 edition of Webster's Dictionary, I found the word *melancholia*, which said, "morbid state of depression; abnormal introspectiveness bordering on insanity." Melancholia, as presented in a dictionary that's more than thirty years old, has a clinical ring to it. Years ago, the severe melancholy state would indeed have been accessed as clinically insane. Today, being intensely introspective is not viewed as "abnormal" or "bordering on insanity."

The Melancholy temperament is a study in contrasts. Melancholy people experience the highest highs and the lowest lows. As well as being very introspective and analytical (sometimes overly so), they're extremely organized and their way of dressing reflects this. They're well-groomed with never a hair out of place. Melancholies have a difficult time relaxing and having fun. They're list-makers who take themselves and others very seriously. They usually take a superior attitude, probably because they have such depth of thought. In their eyes, other people cannot keep up.

Melancholies, as already noted, are easily depressed and sometimes have to guard against negative thinking. This is why they are prone to depression. Melancholies are too easily hurt; they're inclined to take everything too personally, even when something isn't about them. They've been known to read a deep, hidden meaning into each casual comment. Consequently, they're generally ill at ease in social situations.

Take the Four Temperament Personality Indicator!

I'd like to encourage you to turn to Appendix IV at this juncture. Here you'll find the Four Temperament Personality Indicator. For our forgiveness work later, it'll be important to know what temperament you might favor. Of course, as with the sensory modes, remember not to compartmentalize. You may find that you're a mixture of two temperaments. Usually, one of the four will be the most dominant.

If you have chosen to take the temperament profile in Appendix IV and have taken the sensory mode test in Appendix III, you've just participated in what had been Phase II of my study. You're also getting a clearer picture of how you respond to the world around you and how you best process information.

Results of Phase II of the Study

I'd also like to encourage you at this point to turn to Appendix V for the final piece of this huge puzzle that we can use as a dynamic tool for inner healing. These are the results of the findings of Phase II of the Study. The results of Phase II prove that the sensory mode you lead with, coupled with your temperament, will determine to what degree you'll internalize abuse or what you perceive as abuse, how you'll deal with it, and how difficult it'll be to get past it.

So, go ahead and take a quick peek at Appendix V. The rest of what I have to say on the matter will make more sense to you after you do. We'll resume this discussion when you get back…

Now that you've read Appendix V, let's talk about what all those facts and figures actually mean. In terms of the four temperaments and the three sensory modes, they mean that Melancholies and Kinesthetics, by way of their very nature, would be more prone than anyone else to internalize abuse.

If you place a sanguine child and a melancholy child in the same abusive classroom situation, the melancholy child will be more likely to internalize the situation and intensify it for themselves. The sanguine child may be more concerned with talking and having fun with peers instead of spending much time dwelling on an abusive situation. One sarcastic remark from a nun such as "You must be very hard for God to love" may set up a melancholy child for a lifetime of low self-esteem, while the same remark delivered to a sanguine child would merely be laughed at and forgotten.

It's not that the Melancholy is a prime target for abuse. I don't mean to imply that we should blame the victim in these circumstances. If the essence of this book is about forgiveness, it's also about taking responsibility for the various personality traits that make us more vulnerable and more receptive to abuse than others. As adults, we need to recognize that we may have suffered greatly as children because of these vulnerabilities and susceptibilities. Yes, we may have been exposed to the seeds of fear, shame and guilt; however, it's because of our individual personalities that we possess the fertile ground for such seeds to grow. Realizing this can help bring us to a place of forgiveness so that we can move on in our lives.

Knowledge of your Preferred Sensory System Can Help Heal!

We've already touched on the three different sensory modes. They actually represent the three different ways in which people learn. We've talked about the visual, auditory, and kinesthetic sensory modes. We know that people who favor the visual mode learn about the world primarily through their sense of sight. Auditory people glean their knowledge mostly from what they hear being said.

Vulnerability of the Kinesthetic Sensory Mode

When we are operating in our kinesthetic sensory mode, we are much more vulnerable to abuse.

This is because when we are in our kinesthetic mode, we are accessing our feelings. We are being particularly vulnerable and emotionally sensitive. When you're really in touch with your feelings, you are operating from your kinesthetic mode.

Kinesthetics are emotional and introspective. When they're feeling on top of things, they're flying high. When they feel bad, they sink lower than low. There's always the danger of depression for a kinesthetic person.

The fact that kinesthetics are introspective people doesn't mean that they're emotionally withdrawn. They are very intuitive. They can sense when they're in trouble and should back off.

The way that you can tell they are operating in their kinesthetic mode in that moment is that their eyes are cast downward. If a person's gaze is down a good deal of the time, this is always a good clue that they're primarily kinesthetic people.

But Wait; There's More!

We've learned that the most vulnerable of the four temperaments is Melancholy and the most vulnerable of the three sensory modes is Kinesthetic. We've talked about the fact that people who are operating in their melancholy temperament and/or their kinesthetic sensory modes would therefore be more susceptible to internalizing abuse or what they perceive as abuse.

Referring back to our earlier point about changing the rules in the Catholic Church, if people felt as though they'd been abandoned, perhaps their temperament and/or preferred sensory mode may have influenced those feelings.

Healing from Deep Traumatic Abuse

So, what about the child who was gravely wronged? I don't mean a child subjected to just a sarcastic remark. I'm referring to a molestation or rape. Such an atrocity is a major invasion of physical, emotional, and sexual boundaries and can rob a child of sweet innocence and a carefree childhood.

If you're among the many people who've had such a tragedy happen to you as a child, there is hope of healing your wounds. I can imagine that you may be livid at the suggestion of letting go of the anger or devastation you may be carrying around, whether it be aimed at the parochial school, an individual who taught you there, the Catholic Church, or even God. You may still be grieving very much over a lost childhood that you can never regain.

Part of that grieving includes feeling the anger. Remember to allow yourself to feel your feelings. The only way out is through! You may have just opened a whole can of worms with all of this denial-breaking. Remember to journal about any feelings that come up and release them by sharing them with a trusted friend. In the chapters that follow, we'll start doing some other experiential exercises to help move through the grieving part of the journey toward healing.

OBSESSIVE-COMPULSIVE DISORDER

There is still one more component of a person's personality that, if present, can contribute to a more difficult time processing abuse, and that can amplify internalization of abuse. The knowledge of the presence of this component and the way that it operates can be another piece of the puzzle for you. I am speaking of Obsessive-Compulsive Disorder.

If you have a predisposition to Obsessive-Compulsive Disorder, (OCD) then a strict, black-and-white atmosphere such as the old Catholic School system can prove to be a breeding ground for trouble. OCD is a genetic condition which by its very nature is ritualistic. To quote from an old psychiatric textbook, *Patterns and Meaning in Psychiatric Patients* by I.M. Marks, M.D., (1965):

> "In 1878, Dr. Westphal was attributed with the first definition of OCD." ...[It is defined as] "ideas which come to consciousness in spite of and contrary to the will of the patient and which he is unable to suppress although he recognizes them as abnormal and not characteristic of himself."

To give you an example of this definition, I'll share the experiences of one of the people I interviewed who has OCD. We will call her "Janet." Janet's experience is indicative of only one facet of the condition of OCD.

It seems that, as a child growing up in a parochial school, Janet was plagued by spontaneous thoughts (or visions) of a penis every time she attended Mass at her church. This especially happened during what is known in the Roman Catholic dogma as the Offertory. (This is the segment of the Mass when the priest consecrates the host. Catholics believe that, during the Offertory, the bread and wine are truly changed into the body and blood of Jesus.) When the priest raised the host, Janet would involuntarily think of or see a penis.

The explanation as to why a penis, of all things, would be the thought and/or vision Janet would involuntarily conjure up is clear. She was being brought up in a school system that gave overt or covert messages that a boy's penis was bad or dirty. Also, she was being raised in a system which preached heavily about "impure thoughts" and temptations. Dr. Westphal's definition of OCD states that the thought or idea comes to the conscious mind in spite of the will of the person, and that the person is unable to suppress this thought or idea. This would explain the reason Janet's object was something she perceived as taboo, in this case, a penis. When a person has OCD, they're literally a slave to things they don't want to do.

Again referring to the aforementioned textbook, *Patterns of Meaning in Psychiatric Patients*, Dr. Lewis, in speaking about the OCD patient, says that the more the person tries to suppress the thought or obsession, the worse it can become. He says the effort is always in vain.

> "It is like a mental calculus... The intruder may be a thought, an idea, an image or an impulse. Mostly the obsessive content is unpleasant; occasionally it is meaningless. Very rarely is it pleasant."

Using my own history as an example, it's easy to see why I had the episode with picking up the lint in my bedroom. I was suffering from a bad case of scruples so I thought everything I did was a sin. I didn't want any part of the host to be on the floor because I was taught that would be a sin. Additionally, I had a mild case of obsessive-compulsive disorder at the time.

The term *obsessive* refers to the repetitive thought that cannot be escaped, in this case that I was going to Hell if I didn't make sure the floor was free of any particle of the communion host. The term *compulsive* refers to the impulse to complete the action, in this case, to get every piece of whatever was on the floor that might be part of the host. All this is bizarre thinking to a "normal" human being, yet for people with OCD, this type of mental torment goes on daily. Moreover, it is fueled by guilt and shame.

Every sufferer of OCD is literally a slave to his or her obsessions and compulsions. Many OCD sufferers are compelled to perform numerous and very bizarre rituals before leaving the house. For instance, compulsive hand washers must wash their hands repeatedly a certain number of times. Maybe they've decided that number should be twenty-four, fifty-six or eighty. They engage in this ritual many times in one day. If they don't, they truly believe that something bad will happen. Others with OCD are involved in bizarre rituals such as having to walk a certain amount of steps from the bathroom to the kitchen. If they're interrupted by the telephone they'll have to start all over again. Or, if they complete the task in just one step less than or more than the number they themselves have set, they'll have to start the entire process over again. These people are known as the counters.

Then, there are the checkers. They need to check and re-check to make sure something is done. From time to time, we've all had the uneasy feeling that we've gone away from the house and left the water running or a door unlocked. With OCD, if the thought comes to the sufferer's mind that they had left the door unlocked, that thought becomes an obsession. They feel compelled to go home and check, but not just once. Upon returning home, checking and finding the door locked, they feel momentarily satisfied. They get into the car and start to drive again. Additional obsessive thoughts ensue and eventually they turn the car around, to go home and recheck.

Many times people who don't exhibit any of the strange symptoms and bizarre rituals of OCD are persons with obsessions and compulsions to excessively eat, drink, gamble, shop, etc. Let's make the distinction between obsessive-compulsive disorder and obsessive-compulsive behavior. The two are similar to the extent that both types of people may feel they have a problem that they cannot stop. The similarity ends there because, while the latter cannot stop their gambling, shopping in excess, etc., they do perceive these activities to be pleasurable if done in moderation.

In their book, *Obsessive Compulsive Disorders: Theory and Management* (1992), Michael Jenike M.D., Lee Baer, Phd., and William Manichiello tell us that there is a biochemical imbalance of the brain in people with OCD. They write:

> "Alterations in one or more brain chemical systems that regulate repetitive behaviors may be related to the cause of OCD." Further, they tell us that "psychological factors and stress may heighten symptoms and that it is now estimated that 2%-3% of the population may suffer from OCD at some point in their lives."

Getting back to Janet

Janet had also stated that in addition to OCD, she had also suffered from a bad case of scruples born out of the guilt she carried from being a sex abuse survivor. So now she had the whole confessional drama (much as I did as a child) during which she was plagued with fear and shame with having to confess to a priest what she thought were "impure thoughts." How could she even talk to a priest about penises? But, she felt she had to confess it. And, it must have been a sacrilege to desecrate the host like that...and on and on went her thought process.

Breeding Ground for OCD and Scruples

At this juncture, let me reiterate that I had conducted the Independent Study among Adult Children of Parochial Schools between 1990-1992. Except for edited updates, this book was completed in 1998. Now, in 2012, with an additional fourteen years experience as a psychotherapist specializing in trauma, depression, and addiction, I can tell you that the amount of people out there suffering from OCD is staggering!

The early days of the Catholic school system, as it presented itself to the baby boom generation, was a virtual breeding ground for scruples and a place where any OCD tendencies could flourish because of the fear instilled to keep children under control; because of the guilt tactics used to manipulate certain behaviors, and because of the shame projected onto children if they failed to live up to others' expectations. Certainly this dysfunctional system would be enough to trigger bouts of OCD in children already biochemically predisposed and bring on bizarre rituals and manifestations of the disorder. Tendencies toward OCD will certainly contribute to a person's vulnerability to abuse and inability to process and move through trauma in a healthy manner.

This I know from personal history with my own OCD. I know that it had guilt at its core, because when I stopped feeling guilty and super-analyzing whether something was right or wrong, all the OCD manifestations stopped.

Blaming vs. Taking Responsibility

This brings to mind the old adage, "Which came first, the chicken or the egg?" I used to think (when I was deep into "Victim Thinking") that the Catholic Church's teachings and the parochial school system caused my scruples and OCD rituals. While there were certainly dysfunctional components ingrained within that system that manifested in the use of guilt, shame, and fear tactics, the plain truth was that *I* had OCD *and* part of my temperament *is* Melancholy. While it is true that having OCD and/or a Melancholy temperament are not crimes, I needed to be accountable for *what is*.

When I think back to all the energy I'd wasted in my adult lifetime, blaming the parochial school system for my scruples and for the hell I went through as a child, I wonder how many others have experienced this same misguided channeling of energy. I can reason intellectually that, although the anger I felt at the nuns and priests at my school was certainly justified and a normal part of the grieving I've done over parts of my childhood that were lost, the responsibility of my susceptibility to internalizing abuse was mine. (Note—I didn't say *blame*, I said *responsibility*.)

My susceptibility to internalizing abuse was a product of my personality make-up that included a melancholy personality, preferred kinesthetic sensory mode, and my obsessive-compulsive disorder. When I quit blaming, I began to experience freedom, the release of pent-up tension, and attitude changes.

Blaming is very powerless and subjective. It's a de-energizing stance that one can choose to take or not. The operative word here is CHOICE. The question we need to ask ourselves is "What is the payoff?"

What's the payoff for the anger we feel? What's the advantage of the added weight of the ill feelings and negativity which exist in our psyche? We know that life is not fair, yet every fiber of our being screams to balance the scales. And yet, when all is said and done, who is the one who isn't playing fair when we think of the self-sabotage involved? We are sabotaging our own happiness if we allow a life-long resentment to fester.

But Wait! There is More We Need to Understand!

You can see that we're using our combined knowledge of the four temperaments and the three sensory systems of NLP as tools for inner healing in several ways. We'll continue to do so in the chapters that follow. At this juncture, let's take a look at the driving components that create shame-based people. Then we will look at the motivating forces that might compel abusive people to become teachers and to enter the priesthood, become a nun or a minister. This will shed some light on why sexual abuse among religious leaders has been so prevalent.

Shame-based Society

It's not the traumas we suffer in childhood that make us emotionally ill, but the inability to express those traumas. The inability to express the trauma comes from shame. Shame is supported within our society. This is a shame-based society. Shame is multi-generational.

In *Facing Shame,* Fossum and Mason, (1989) describe toxic shame in this manner:

> "Shame is an inner sense of being completely diminished or insufficient as a person. It is the self judging the self. A moment of shame may be a humiliation so painful or an indignity so profound that one feels one has been robbed of his or her dignity or exposed as basically inadequate, bad or worthy of rejection. A pervasive sense of shame is the ongoing premise that one is fundamentally bad, inadequate, defective, unworthy, or not fully valid as a human being."

When people are shamed as children, they end up acting out that shame in some way and at some point in their lives. The reason shame is easily passed from one generation to another is best explained in *Facing Shame.* This book addresses and identifies the presence of intense shame and other unusually overwhelming feelings in victims of child abuse. Adult victims of abuse seem to experience shame, pain, fear and anger more intensely than normal healthy adults do. This is because, as children, they had picked up the strong feelings of shame, pain, fear or anger from their abusers during the abusive experiences. It is as if the abusers were somehow inducing the feelings into the children. The children were absorbing the feelings like a sponge. (Boundaries are a learned thing; children do not come out of the womb with boundaries.) In turn, the children then carried these induced feelings forward into their lives. With this concept in mind, it is quite conceivable, then, that generations of people would be affected by carried shame, guilt, fear and anger.

How Schools Can Become a Set-Up for Toxic Shame

I asked a colleague, L. William Wade, who has specialized in the dynamic and interplay within the four temperaments for two decades, how education systems, particularly within any religious dogmatic movement, can become a setting for toxic shame. He had this to say:

> "Schools, just like any other institution, are obviously founded by people who are leaders. We look at our nation's history and the founding fathers were leaders who fought against the establishment. These kinds of people have vision and they believe in what they do. Often times, these individuals have tendencies and traits that we would identify as Choleric. You would not necessarily find a Melancholy striking out on their own with their own belief system as passionately or as often as Cholerics do. Cholerics, by their very nature, are people who get an idea or plan in their head and then they set out to accomplish that plan. Our system in America was established because people wanted religious freedom. That religious freedom was desired by those who did not want to knuckle under to others telling them what to do. We see a Choleric trait in wanting to tell others what to do; they would not want others telling them what to do."

> "And so, in one sense we look at our founding fathers and we find that they possess a lot of leadership qualities which are found in Cholerics. These are the type of people who would forego everything because their determination and sheer will is so powerful. Also, by their very nature, Cholerics like to take control; give commands; be in charge. As a result of that, you would find that a Choleric would be more inclined to be in charge of an institution or start one, than you would any of the other temperaments. A Phlegmatic would not have the energy to get something like that going; a Melancholy would see all the difficulties in starting a system or an institution; a Sanguine would not have the drive or dedication to put in the hours needed; they'd spend more time talking instead of getting things done."

Chapter V. Understanding as a Resource for Healing

"A Choleric's life-theme is work, and their nature is to want to control and give people orders. Therefore you have dynamic and powerful people in types of jobs where they're able to give instructions to other people. Police departments, office managers and governments are filled with choleric individuals. All these people like to tell others what to do. They're usually good at administration and they usually have the tenacity to accomplish things. They don't know what it means to quit."

"In discussing the issue of discipline, Cholerics often are very stern disciplinarians and because they are, would not be very compassionate to others who disobey the rules. So, in a setting where they're giving people orders, they would not treat a sensitive Melancholy child, for example, with much compassion. Of the four temperaments, Cholerics are least prone to compassion; tears turn them off. They don't like tears or sensitivity. Nor do they like people who don't go along with them. So, if you want to get along with a Choleric, you have to follow what it is they like to do. Don't ask any questions and when you're responding to them, always respond in a matter-of-fact manner; short and abbreviated."

"Something to consider in dealing with the early parochial school system is that people who have grown up to become nuns, priests, and/or teachers may have, themselves, come from a harsh, strict home. This could have given them a desire to be in control themselves, consequently they would seek out careers or vocations that allowed them to be in control. An example would be a nun who grew up with a harsh and abusive father. It is quite conceivable that she may not want to get married because of the father's abuse and yet she may want to give people orders. This would be a natural segue into becoming a nun."

"There were very few jobs in the 40's-60's which afforded a woman the capability to give commands and be in charge of people, and certainly school teaching was one that was accepted and would legitimize over-use of power. Power corrupts and absolute power corrupts absolutely. Therefore, we could possibly extrapolate that a nun who had been in a difficult home life or that was Choleric-oriented and was given power in the beginning of her career and had allowed that power to go unchecked, could allow her power to eat on itself in time. Power needs accountability. If there is no accountability, power runs amok."

Thank you, L. William Wade! Now, tie in Mr. Wade's observations on what happens when shame-based people and/or choleric people (who gravitate toward the teaching profession) choose to educate and/or become part of the clergy as educators, with what Fossum and Mason say about induced or carried feelings of shame, guilt, fear and anger during abuse. We now begin to get a clear picture of how the stage was set in the early parochial school system. We begin to see why it all happened as it did. We begin to understand why so many adults today find it hard to work through feelings of shame, guilt, fear and anger that were inflicted upon them by shame-based people during abuse and that were also used as teaching tools.

The picture takes on even a clearer focus when we recognize the target of these carried feelings is a child who possesses one or more of the components of a Melancholy temperament, a Kinesthetic preferred sensory mode, or an Obsessive-Compulsive Disorder.

There is still one more piece of this puzzle of understanding before we close this chapter. That is the understanding of why sexual abuse among religious leaders has been so prevalent.

Sexual Abuse Among Religious Leaders

For at least the past twenty years, the media has been bombarded with stories of molestations performed by members of the clergy thirty or more years ago. People are coming forward and these stories surface after thirty years of secrecy, as was the aforementioned Father Porter case of North Attleboro, Massachusetts. When the media sheds a light on such atrocities, people are astounded at the very idea that a person who has supposedly dedicated their life to Christ would commit such a desecration against little children and society.

To delve further, we need to take a look at three types of individuals. They are the person addicted to religion, the sexually compulsive person, and those who have been abused physically and/or sexually.

Religion Addicts

People addicted to religion, obviously, are people who use religion as a drug. They derive solace in their religious practices to the point of compulsion, much like the compulsive overeater does with food or the alcoholic does with alcohol. Acting on a compulsion to do good, religion addicts might be drawn to the helping professions such as nursing, counseling, teaching. They are, just as naturally, drawn to the religious life.

Sex Addicts

A lot of sexually compulsive people are drawn to careers that focus on human relations, especially in the field of morality. It's not uncommon for them to be involved in some aspect of the military or in a religious life, frequently where they counsel others. They also may gravitate toward a profession where they have the opportunity to work with other people's bodies. All this is due to the fact that, while not on a cognizant level, the sexually compulsive person is always seeking out ways in which to be involved with the addiction, in a controlled environment. They may be also trying to use their careers as a defense. In essence, they are saying, "how can there be a problem here, when I'm an expert in my field?"

Cross-Addiction: Religion Addicts/ Sex Addicts

Many times a religion addiction can create a sexually compulsive person or vice versa. In the latter scenario the sexually compulsive person, recognizing that his behavior has gotten out of hand, turns to God for help. However, being an addictive personality, he substitutes the "God thing" for the "sex thing" and becomes cross-addicted. It's either lots of God or lots of sex, in other words, the black or white/feast or famine trait of the addictive personality.

We've already established that an addiction is anything in excess which alters one's mood. A typical cross-addictive behavior, where one flip-flops back and forth from compulsive God stuff (such as reciting the rosary five times a day or going to church twice a day, seven days a week), to compulsive sex stuff (such as having to engage in sex three times a day, seven days a week in order to get a "high" and mask depression) would cycle something like this:

The sex addict, wanting to change and realizing they are being a detriment to themselves and society, desperately seeks solace in God. However, without the aide of counseling or a solid spiritual system such as a Twelve Step program, they cannot come out of the compulsive mode. Being an addictive personality, they substitute one addiction for another. They go along fine for awhile on a "high" with the excessive God stuff. Then one day, something happens to allow their already skewed perception to shift. Either they think God is angry with them or they get angry with God or they make it too hard on themselves to keep God in their life. But being an addictive personality, they still feel the need for a "fix" so it's back to the sex thing in excess.

Physical and Sexual Abuse Survivors

Because abuse survivors many times end up "acting out" the abusive behavior at some point in their lives, people who had been physically abused in their childhood are drawn to fields where violence is a controlled component, such as law enforcement or the military. Remember, people with Choleric temperaments are drawn to these fields as well. The parochial school system of old, with its "spare the rod, spoil the child" mentality, provides an opportunity for the Cholerics, with their controlling and sometimes insensitive nature, to practice controlling legitimately. It also allows physical abuse survivors to slip into a profession which provides an opportunity to "act out" the abuse done to them.

Often, people who have been abused physically have also been abused sexually. It's a known fact that sexual abuse survivors often grow up to "act out" their behavior. Sometimes, they act out their behavior by becoming sex abusers themselves. Couple that with the scenario of the cross-addicted religion-sex compulsion, put that person in the profession of clergy/teacher, which is something that they would be drawn to, and you can understand better how and why sex abuse among religious leaders has happened many times over the years.

DISCLAIMER!

At this point I want to provide a disclaimer. I am NOT saying that every single nun or priest in the parochial school system was or is presently molesting children. They are not. The purpose of this book is NOT to bash any religious institution, but rather to empower the reader to move forward, heal and forgive.

LET'S WRAP IT UP!

Wow! I don't know about you, but I need a break from all this "heady" stuff!

This has been a very enlightening chapter. We've learned a lot about temperament and preferred sensory modes. We've learned how possessing a combination of any or all three of these components—melancholy temperament, kinesthetic sensory mode, and/or Obsessive-Compulsive Disorder—can contribute to a greater susceptibility to internalizing abuse and make it extremely difficult to let go of that abuse.

Further, we've looked at shame as a societal illness and saw what can happen when shame-based people choose the religious life and/or choose to educate.

In Chapter Six, we're going to begin implementing some of the inner resources for healing that I've been discussing. You'll see how coming out of denial, becoming aware, yearning and understanding can help you to move through your grief to a place of forgiveness. You'll begin to reclaim the sweetness and innocence of your youth.

What to Remember After Reading Chapter V:

- Embrace whatever personality type is part of you!

- Each temperament has its own strengths and weaknesses.

- We all need each other to balance our strengths and weaknesses.

- Embrace the unique way in which you learn.

- The way in which you experience the world can be very exciting, whether your experience is visual, auditory or kinesthetic.

- If the section on Obsessive-Compulsive Disorder applies to you, be gentle with yourself. You can ask for and receive professional help with this. If this does not apply to you, be grateful and have compassion for people who know this as a way of life.

Chapter V Affirmation:

"I am loveable and worthwhile just the way I am!"

Chapter VI

You're Too Old to Play Victim Anymore: Formula for Getting Rid of Victim Thinking

Chapter VI
You're Too Old to Play Victim Anymore: Formula for Getting Rid of Victim Thinking

In the last chapters, you've gotten an understanding of the framework and mindset of the earlier religious school systems. For those of you who've been struggling with issues that came from your parochial school days, this is vital information. If you're going to recover from the trauma of those earlier days, you must first shine a bright light on the dynamics of that old dysfunctional system. This uncovering will contribute greatly to understanding, and the understanding can be used as one of your inner resources for healing.

You have also gotten some insights into experiences of other people who went to parochial school. You may have experienced a sense of connection with some of these people; a sense that you weren't alone in your hopeless little spot in Hell. This chapter will implement this new knowledge and understanding.

As children growing up in this (or any dysfunctional) system, we all felt hopeless and desperate. It was a helpless feeling, as we told ourselves that no matter what we did, we were certain to go to Hell for it, and there were no stops in Purgatory, either. There's strength in knowing that we weren't the only ones scared to death of the confessional.

What a load to carry around for such a little person! It is no wonder that, as adults, we suffer so greatly from major back pain and complications! When our bones were growing to house an adult frame, we heaped the extra weight of guilt, shame and anguish upon them.

As you know, children are very creative. It's both refreshing and inspiring to watch children playing. Their imaginations take them soaring; they visit magical territory in their minds. If you dust off those good childhood memories, you'll find a lot of wisdom with which to implement healing. Your inner child can teach you a lot.

The Refrigerator Game

As a child, I had a favorite game that I played with my brothers and cousins called the "Refrigerator Game." Since I'm a visual person by nature, I can still see my brothers and all our cousins in my mind's eye. I remember how they looked, and even where they sat as we played this game in our grandparents' family room. You may have played this game or a variation of it.

If you haven't, let me describe how it's played:

Everyone sits in close proximity, usually a circle. The first person starts with, "In my refrigerator there is/are_____" (naming something starting with the letter A. It doesn't necessarily have to be edible). The person sitting next to the first person then says, "In my refrigerator there is/are_____" (repeats the A word just given and adds an item beginning with the letter B). The third person says, "In my refrigerator there is/are_____" (repeats A and B words) "and _____" (adds a word beginning with C). The game continues with each person until the entire alphabet is used. It keeps going around the circle over again, so that it becomes a memory game.

I've been using this game in many of my seminars for years because it serves two purposes. First, it's a great icebreaker to get people talking to each other. Second, it's a tool for getting in touch with the particular sensory system a person is using for remembering. In fact, it's an excellent tool to learn how you remember things.

After playing this within the context of my lectures and workshops, I help each participant evaluate the experience.

Chapter VI. You're Too Old to Play Victim Anymore

I ask them to think about how they remembered each item mentioned in the game when it was their turn. Did they have to look at each individual person, as they recalled what that person said? Or, did they recall a picture of what was said for each letter of the alphabet?

For instance, if *banana* had been used for the letter B, did Dave picture in his mind a bunch of bananas and associate it with the person who said it? Or, did Dave associate each face in the circle with the item that person had named?

Maybe John used a different strategy to remember in this game. Possibly he had to say the alphabet to himself (or hear himself sing it as he did in Kindergarten) in order to remember the items in the refrigerator.

Still another way to remember is how Nick did it. He got a sense of what came next, without having to tune in to any pictures or alphabet reciting.

By now, you probably realize that I'm talking about NLP again—communicating and receiving communication by one of the three major sensory modes, or a combination of the three. In the first example, Dave remembered the correct sequence of items mentioned by looking at each person. Obviously he was operating visually. After looking at a person, if he had then sensed the item that person had mentioned, Dave would have been using his kinesthetic mode, second to his visual mode. His strategy for remembering in this case would be Visual to Kinesthetic.

For another example, perhaps the player had to look at each person in order to remember something the person had *said* pertaining to their item. For instance, if it was Louis' turn and he looked at Sandra and then remembered that Sandra had said, "pizza" [for the letter p] "because my Aunt Lillian is coming to visit," then Louis would know the strategy he had used for remembering was Visual to Auditory, because he first "got it" by *seeing* Sandra, which caused him to recall what she had *said*.

Perhaps while playing the game, Janice had to say the alphabet silently to herself each time it was her turn, in conjunction with looking at the players first. It would be clear, then, that the strategy she had used for remembering was Visual to Auditory, because she was cueing herself by <u>listening</u> after <u>seeing.</u> But, what if she could not look at anybody in order to hear the alphabet clearly? Then, Janice would be operating strictly in her auditory mode and any attempt at visuals would be a distraction.

Suppose that when it was Alexa's turn, she amazed herself at just being able to get a feel for what came next in succession without looking at anyone or hearing any alphabet? Only occasionally did she get stuck and have to look up at a person. This means Alexa's strategy for remembering in the game was kinesthetic with a visual back-up.

Why not play this the very next time you get the opportunity to be in a group? Try it with your family. Later, after you've played, you can use this to evaluate your own method of playing. You may discover, upon evaluating your own method of playing that you have a definite pattern. You may use all three modalities to remember, you may use just two, or perhaps just one modality is dominant. Whatever you discover, remember your strategy for this game.

I offer for your consideration that the same strategy you used for remembering will best serve you for forgiving. For, in order to forgive, you first have to remember. The sensory system (or combination of sensory systems) that you use for remembering will prove to be your sharpest for the forgiveness work presented later in this book.

One last thought about playing this game. Never tell the real reason for playing the game (tapping into your personal strategy for remembering) until the game is over. It works best in retrospect. I never tell my participants until after we've played it. If they are aware beforehand, the recall process won't be spontaneous.

Looking at our Inner Resources

We've laid the groundwork with this memory game. Now we'll begin to enumerate our plan of action for healing trauma. In doing so, visual people will be able to see a step-by-step plan for recovery. Those of you whose strategy for learning is kinesthetic will get a sense of order because there is a definite step-by-step procedure. And, to you auditory people, I have a real clear suggestion for you: copy the following list of Inner Resources for Healing Trauma. Read it out loud to yourself, listen to your voice, and hear what you are saying.

I've outlined the Inner Resources for Healing Trauma. Afterwards, we'll explore each one. I usually write these on a white-board or do a power point presentation at a seminar so that the visual people can see them and the kinesthetic people can get a sense of order or direction. The auditory people will rely mostly on what they hear me say. What is written on the board will only be secondary to them. Now "let's go to the board" and chart our route.

Inner Resources for Healing Trauma

I. Knowledge of three ways we learn
   A. Visual Sensory Mode
   B. Auditory Sensory Mode
   C. Kinesthetic Sensory Mode

II. Formula for Getting Rid of Victim Thinking
   A. Awareness
      1. Negative thoughts
      2. Victim sentences"
   B. Utilize dominant sensory system
      1. To stop yourself
      2. In breathing exercises
      3. To take charge

    C. Sentence Reversal

    D. Sensory Affirmation exercise

    E. Sensory Escape exercise

    F. Sensory Journaling exercise

III. Forgive the Past

    A. Understanding

    B. Experiential Exercises

    C. Abandonment issues

    D. Grieving our losses

IV. Redefine Success for Yourself

We've already covered Number I—the sensory modalities we use to learn. So let's turn our attention to Number II—Victim Thinking. Victim Thinkers hold the belief system that they are enslaved by their set of life circumstances and are powerless over things that "happen to me." The key to alleviating Victim Thinking is mastering one's life. I call Victim Thinking "The Killer."

We can start our understanding of Victim Thinking with a joke:

The "Poop" Joke

Twenty-seven years ago, when I was very heavily into my Victim Thinking, I heard a joke that I absolutely loved telling because it really spoke to my choice to be a victim. Maybe you've heard this one:

> A man died and went to Hell. In Hell, the man met a demon. This demon told the man that he got to choose his own punishment. He got to pick what was behind Door #1, Door #2, or Door #3. The man thought that sounded pretty good, considering he was in Hell and all. So, he asked the demon to show him what was behind Door #1. The demon opened the door and the man saw hundreds of people standing on their

heads on a wooden floor. "Well," the man told the demon, "I can't stand on my head on a wooden floor for eternity. Let me see what's behind Door #2." So, the demon opened Door #2 for the man. There the man saw hundreds of people standing on their heads on a cement floor. Now, the man was getting very indignant. "I can't stand on my head for eternity here either. Cement is worse than wood! What is behind Door #3?" So the demon opened Door #3. The man saw thousands of people behind Door #3 and they were having a ball! They were laughing, eating, smoking, telling stories, singing and drinking. But, there was one problem. They were standing in poop up to their knees! "Well," the man said, holding his nose, "I don't want to stand in poop for eternity, but they look like they're having a good time. I'll take Door #3." The demon let him in and shut the door. Just then, another demon came in, blew a whistle and said, "OK, break time is over. Everyone back on your heads!"

That's my poop joke. You can see that it really supported my feeling that life stunk! And worse, I was going to be a victim in death, as well. I still love that joke and tell it often. But today I love it for another reason. Now, instead of feeling smug and indignant and like "poor me," I can laugh at it and see how far I've come.

I'd like to share with you a formula I created for myself that really worked for me. It's based on sentence reversal and my knowledge of NLP. We're going to rely heavily on our sensory skills to make this work!

My formula for Stamping out Victim Thinking:

1. Be Aware
2. Breathe
3. Sensory Stop and Take Charge Exercise
4. Sentence Reversal
5. Sensory Affirmation Exercise
6. Sensory Escape Exercise
7. Sensory Journaling Exercise

1. Be Aware of Victim Sentences

Many times during the day we've all caught ourselves in the middle of a victim sentence. I'll give you a really easy example: "The rain woke me up." When I say this sentence I'm implying that I had absolutely no power of choice in the matter. It was me vs. the rain, and the rain won! With the very structure of the sentence, I actually set myself up to be a victim. Do you hear the powerlessness in that sentence? "The rain woke me up." You can hear the powerlessness; you can see the powerlessness; you can sense the powerlessness. By thinking or saying, "The rain woke me up," I'm giving away a great deal of my power.

By changing the sentence, or sometimes reversing it, you can free yourself from the stance of victim. Ask yourself what it would take to regain your power in the sentence, "The rain woke me up?" What if you took the action first, instead of reacting? Consciously reverse the sentence so that it reads, "I heard the sound of the rain on the windowpane and I woke up." There. Now, you had a choice in the matter. You weren't the rain's poor victim.

Now let's concentrate on a few exercises to really stamp out the victim thinking in your life. Call to mind some of the victim thoughts you've allowed in your life. Remember some of the negative emotions, visions, thoughts, sounds or feelings that make up the victim thinking in your life. Now create a sentence that encapsulates some of this negative victim thinking. You might decide to phrase a victim sentence about an experience you had in the religious school system you attended.

For example, "Sister Mary Genuflexia made me feel stupid." Or you might decide to think of a negative sentence you use to tell yourself that you cannot attain your goal. For example, "I know I'll never get that promotion because I'm not smart enough."

Whatever surfaces for you, use it. You'll find that it isn't necessary to think too hard. Whatever is most important to you will surface. Write anything that comes to your mind that is a victim sentence. After you've done that, look at the sentence. Do you see the powerlessness in this sentence? Say it out loud. Hear the powerlessness. Get a sense of how this powerlessness feels. Now, set aside your victim sentence for a short time. We will come right back to it.

2. Breathe!

As trite as this may sound, we must remind ourselves to breathe. When you recognize yourself in the midst of a life-draining negative thought or a victim sentence, instead of beating yourself up, be kind and gentle to yourself! Acknowledge yourself for starting to become cognizant of distorted thinking in your life. Awareness is the first step necessary in order for change to occur!

3. Sensory Stop and Take Charge Exercise

Right now, I'll give you a script. I suggest you record this onto recording software or a digital recorder. You can use some soft, soothing instrumental music as background, if that appeals to you. Speak slowly and clearly, pausing frequently. After you've recorded this script, play it back for yourself.

Here is your script:

> Make yourself as comfortable as possible. Become aware of your breathing as you inhale through your nose and exhale through your mouth. Check to see if there is any tension anywhere in your body. Inhale again and this time bring the air in and focus it on the area with the tension. Now, let go of the tension in your body as you exhale through your mouth. And, as you exhale through your mouth, allow the tension to leave your body. Let go. Let go and relax. Relax and trust. And now, think of the victim sentence that you wrote down. In your mind's eye, picture an octagon-shaped red stop sign being held in front of you. Or picture a big flashing red light. Hear the word *stop* in your mind. Say the word *stop* out loud if necessary. Listen to yourself saying it. Put your name behind it. Listen again. *Stop,*_____(your name). Now, feel yourself

stopping, halting. Feel as a force in your stomach stops you cold. Feel it stopping in your head. Feel the sensation of stopping your negative thinking. Stop!

And now, take charge of yourself. See yourself walking on a crooked path. Up ahead, there is a fork in the road. To the left, the crooked path continues. To the right, the path becomes straight, solid, centered. Make a conscious decision to go to the right. See in your mind's eye the image of yourself taking charge by getting yourself on the straight, centered, solid path. Hear yourself say "I take charge of my life." Say to yourself, using your name, "I,_____, take charge of my life." Say it again. "I,_____, take charge of my life." Feel yourself taking charge of your own life. Get a sense of strength and self-assurance. Feel your power. Feel both your feet solidly on the ground. Feel grounded. Feel centered. Get a sense that you're taking charge of yourself.

Stop recording, rewind, and then listen to the words you've recorded. As you listen, experience the suggestions you've just recorded for yourself.

4. Sentence Reversal

Now let's do a sentence reversal using the sentence you wrote a few minutes ago. Let's change the words of the sentence so that you're not in a powerless stance. By changing the words of the sentence, you take charge. You have lost your powerlessness. You have mastery of yourself and your body and mind will heal. For instance, the sentence given earlier, "Sister Mary Genuflexia made me feel stupid" can be reversed to read, "I heard what Sister Mary Genuflexia said about me and I told myself something that made me feel stupid." Do you see the difference? By reversing it, you're no longer a victim in the situation.

The important thing to remember is that no one can make you feel any certain way except you. You can react to what someone is saying and decide to feel bad about it, but no one can get inside your feelings. Although someone's behavior may indeed create the *impetus* for a feeling, it is *your* thought about the behavior that creates the feeling.

Chapter VI. You're Too Old to Play Victim Anymore

For example, if someone is offering to help me mow the lawn, my thought about their offer to help might be, "they don't think I can do it!" In that case, I might feel hurt or angry. But, suppose after they had offered to help me mow the lawn, my thought had been, "what a nice gesture." Then, I would probably be very happy about the offer. We can look at a person's behavior and our feeling about the behavior. But, in between their behavior and our feeling, there is always a thought. Again, what we think creates our feeling.

As a child, you were helpless and you didn't know these things. Now, you can make different choices. When you're aware of your victim sentences and you decide to reverse them, you're taking charge of yourself and mastering your life.

As I mentioned earlier, negative emotions can depress the immune system. When you take control by reversing your victim sentences, you're contributing to good health because you'll feel centered and calm instead of out of control.

Allow people to have their own perceptions and thoughts about you. It's not realistic to assume that every person in your life will absolutely love everything you do and say one hundred per cent of the time. When you allow other people to have their opinions about you, you've freed yourself of a lot of stress because you don't react to their words. When you react to what people say, you're powerless. By allowing them their opinions, you once again have power. You can take control of your own life.

Try not to react to what you perceive as being a negative remark toward you. Identify your feelings. If you're feeling angry, recognize that feeling and let it run through your body. Without blocking the feelings, let them start from the top of your head and go straight out your toes. (We'll practice doing this with another experiential exercise soon.) If you block the feelings, it will most certainly cause a shut-down of your body. Blocking emotions causes a shut-down of the nervous system and you will either get sick or stay sick. Remember, **negative emotions depress the immune system.**

Without reacting destructively to what people say, walk away. Or, you might say, "That isn't true, and I can't change what you believe." The important thing to remember is that your primary goal is wellness of mind, body and spirit. When you let go of the anger or resentment at a rejecting statement, you will remain calm. It's a fact that this will allow healing energy to flow into your body instead of shutting down your nervous system.

When you're frustrated about a confrontation, it is in the letting go that you relax and heal. Remember that you need to practice loving yourself. Contrary to what we learned as children, this is not a selfish act.

So far we have become cognizant of our negative thinking, reminded ourselves to breathe, and have constructed and reversed a victim sentence. In between, we have used all three sensory systems—visual, auditory, kinesthetic—to receive suggestions to take charge of our lives. We've stopped ourselves from victimization, taken back our power, and taken charge of our thoughts utilizing all three sensory modes.

Now, let's do the Sensory Affirmation exercise. This is an excellent exercise for getting in touch with hidden feelings.

5. Sensory Affirmation Exercise

Let's take time to create an affirmation based on the positive sentence you just wrote. For instance, in our example reversed sentence, "I heard what Sister Mary Genuflexia said about me and I told myself something that made me feel stupid" an affirmation supporting your decision to not be a victim might be, "I,_____, (your name) allow people to think what they wish." Or, how about, "What other people think or say about me does not define who I am."

Any affirmation to reach your goal to eradicate negative thinking from your life will do. Even if you think it doesn't relate to your present issue, use whatever comes up. On a subconscious level, it will relate. Now, write this affirmation out on paper.

After you've written it once, write down beside it the very first thought, word, feeling or sound that you experience. If, after writing your affirmation, you think of how silly you feel, write it down. *I feel silly.* Or, maybe what will surface for you will be a feeling of frustration. Write down *frustration.* Or, you might see an image of something before your eyes. Write it down. You might become aware of a sound instead of a feeling or image. I once had a very auditory person in one of my seminars who said he heard the sound of a locomotive. If you begin to hear sounds, write them down. Now, drop down a line and write the affirmation again. Next to it, write whatever surfaces for you again. Do this ten times.

Now, let's go back to your recording device. You can record the following script at the end of the first script we did.

6. Sensory Escape Exercise

Be aware of your breathing. Allow any tension in your body to be felt. Take a deep breath through your nose. Release the tension as you exhale through your mouth. Continue to breathe deeply. (*Pause here as you breathe for a few minutes.*) If any negative feelings have surfaced in these exercises, allow these negative feelings to run through your body. Decide whether you can best see, hear, or feel this negativity. If you could see all this negativity, what would it look like? Maybe a big black cloud or a red, fiery ball or a steel pendulum or whatever you want to see. Picture your symbol of negativity getting bigger and bigger and coming closer and closer to you. If you've made the decision to let yourself hear this negativity, if hearing works best for you, what does this negativity sound like? Maybe a shrill whistle or the sound of a fingernail running down a chalkboard or anything you've decided this negativity should sound like. Hear this annoying sound getting louder and louder and more and more annoying to you. If you've decided that what works for you is to experience the negativity as unpleasant sensations or feelings, let these sensations feel stronger and stronger. Maybe you are experiencing these unpleasant sensations as discomfort in your stomach or tension at the back of your neck.

Now let these pictures or sounds or feelings run through your body. Just relax and let them run through. Feel it. See it. Hear it. Let that sound or image or feeling escape with every breath that you breathe out. Where is the negativity? Where do you see it? Where do you hear it? Where do you feel it? Is it in your chest? Your stomach? Your neck? Your lower back? Wherever you are experiencing this negativity in your body, let it move along and escape with every breath you take. Let it escape through your mouth with every exhale. Let it escape out your toes. It's there. Don't deny it. Denying causes blocking. It's there. Just let it run through your body. Now, let go. Let go of all the negative sensations, all the negative feelings. Let go with every breath out. Continue to breathe slowly and evenly. Let go. Let go and relax. Relax and trust.

Rewind the recording device to the beginning of the Sensory Escape Exercise you just recorded. Get comfortable, take a deep breath and experience it as it plays back.

7. Sensory Journaling Exercise

During these exercises, whatever images, sounds and/or feelings that surfaced are very important. If you've never journaled before, now is the time. As you already know, journaling is writing down your feelings. You can write about events in your life, but keep focusing on the feelings you're experiencing surrounding these events. Pretty soon, what's in your heart and soul will appear on paper.

I believe that very often, when people have a rough time getting in touch with their feelings during journaling, there's a good reason and that reason gets overlooked. People wonder, "What is wrong with me? I write and write but the feelings won't come." I believe this is because, very simply, these people are probably in their visual or auditory mode. At the moment, they're not coming from their kinesthetic (feelings) mode. Nothing is wrong with them. This is why the Sensory Affirmation and the Sensory Escape exercises we just did are important. This kind of sensory work speaks to everyone, regardless of the sensory language a person happens to be using at the time. This has

Chapter VI. You're Too Old to Play Victim Anymore

helped me for years and I've seen it help many clients in my private practice, in the workshops I've facilitated and with the patients I've seen in three different inpatient treatment centers. So I know these exercises will work for you, too!

Keep this exercise handy. As soon as you are comfortable doing so, journal about whatever words you wrote at the end of the affirmations. Suppose your victim sentence was, "Father Martin made me feel like I was going to go to hell for_____." Suppose further that in constructing your reversal sentence, you came up with, "I heard Father Martin tell us we were bad and I internalized it by thinking I'd go to Hell." You have shown yourself that you indeed had a choice in what you thought and in doing so you've reclaimed your power. A good affirmation to coincide with the above reversed sentence might be "I,_____, (your name) am a worthwhile and good person and God loves me just as I am."

Maybe the first time you wrote your affirmation, it was hard to write. The first thing that surfaced was a feeling of disgust, so that is what you put down on your paper beside that affirmation. OK. Fine. Now, write about it. Find out what that disgust is all about. Is it about disbelief that you are a good person or that God loves you?

Here's another example: suppose that the second time you wrote that affirmation, what surfaced wasn't a feeling but a vivid picture of a little child burning in Hell. Write about it. This is your guilt speaking to you through your visual sensory system. Address it.

Are you getting a clear picture of what we're after here? You can go back to it again tomorrow. Do the entire exercise over. It will become clearer each time. Each time, you will discover more about yourself and you will heal a little more.

Journaling helps to physically lift the negativity out of your body. It is a tremendous release of energy. And, we've taken the journaling one step farther by writing about images, sounds and feelings that might have come up during the Sensory Affirmation exercise. This is why I call our journaling *Sensory Journaling*.

There you have the entire formula for eradicating the negativity in your life. The next time you wish to do this entire six-part exercise, the order in which the material is presented will be most productive to you. Furthermore, it will be more effective the next time you do it because there won't be any stopping to record it. Now that you've experienced these exercises, you've already become more aware of negativity in your life. That awareness is the first step in eliminating Victim Thinking.

HERE IS THE EXPERIENTIAL PART OF OUR FORMULA:

1. Construct a Victim Sentence.
2. Listen to recorded Sensory Stop and Take Charge Exercise (your first script).
3. Sentence Reversal.
4. Sensory Affirmation Exercise.
5. Sensory Escape Exercise (your second script).
6. Sensory Journaling Exercise.

Pay special attention to the sensory cues in the Sensory Escape Exercise that had the most impact on you. Could you best see, hear, or feel the negativity? Remember the sensory system you favored. Having done this exercise, you're probably getting a handle on which sensory system to use for best effect. You've already begun to do the work of reclaiming your power by a simple procedure called Sentence Reversal. Now you can apply your power in the sensory language that is your own. In Part II of this book, we will delve into more sensory work.

Wrapping It Up

In Part I of this book we dug deep to enlighten ourselves and to uncover all the hurtful events we experienced in our parochial school days, knowing that in order to heal ourselves, we'd have to call to mind the original pain.

Chapters II and VI have dealt with introducing the three main sensory systems. You've been using these sensory systems as healing tools. You've recognized childhood insecurities and hurts, borne out of a dysfunctional teaching system, as the source of much pain in your adult life. You've also called forth some very valuable inner resources as you've begun to rid yourself of the victim thinking in your life.

Chapters III, IV and V dealt with the first steps toward forgiving past transgressions—breaking denial, being aware, yearning and understanding.

In Part II of this book, we'll take this understanding and knowledge of the three basic sensory systems, and begin to re-center ourselves. We'll take actual personal experiences from our religious school days and re-create what happened to our benefit, using more sensory work.

Finally, the light will begin to show through from the other side as we take a look at re-defining success for ourselves.

We've laid some of the groundwork for forgiveness. Now we'll go about the work of moving toward forgiveness and a higher level of self-love and acceptance. Our work is cut out for us, but it's revitalizing to think that we each have, inside us, the ability to meet life head-on. We can tap into our inner resources at any time. They've been there all along. No need to look any further than the Tin Man's chest.

Things to Remember After Reading Chapter VI:

- You are in command of your own thoughts!

- You can let go of Victim Thinking!

- You have the power to take charge of your life in a positive way!

- You deserve to think positive thoughts!

- You deserve to feel happiness!

- You deserve to be happy!

- Let people think what they want about you!

- What others think or say about you does not define who you are!

Chapter VI Affirmations:

"I take charge of my life and feel an abundance of love!"

"Good things DO happen to me!"

Part II
Healing Through Forgiveness of the Past

Chapter VII

Your Personal Strategy for Forgiving: What to Do With the Feelings

Chapter VII
Your Personal Strategy for Forgiving: What to Do With the Feelings

This is a very powerful chapter. In this section, I'm going to present very heavy-duty forgiveness work. You'll be introduced to your own personal strategy for forgiving, based on memories of experiences in your past. You will also receive hands-on training in the form of experiential exercises. You will learn a lot as you go so let's get right to it without a lot of preliminaries.

At this juncture, let's re-visit a question from Chapter II:

Why Forgive?

Forgiveness is an act that frees us from the negative influences of past experiences. I believe there is a need for forgiveness in one's life on three levels:

  Spiritual
  Physiological
  Emotional

The Need to Forgive on a Spiritual Level

I believe that forgiveness reconciles the soul. As an example, the Catholic Church has a ritualistic sacrament that used to be referred to as Confession or Penance, and that is now referred to as Reconciliation. During Reconciliation, it is first necessary for one to examine their conscience in order to call to mind the transgressions—sins—that they've committed. Then, of course, the actual releasing comes with a confession to another human being, in this case a priest.

In Twelve-Step Recovery programs, such as Alcoholics Anonymous, a similar "ritual" is performed as part of the recovery program. The fourth step to recovery in this program reads "made a fearless and searching moral inventory of ourselves," and the fifth step is "admitted to God, to ourselves and to another human being, the exact nature of our wrongs" (Alcoholics Anonymous Big Book, 1984 addition).

The founding fathers of the Catholic Church and of Alcoholics Anonymous knew the importance and benefits of humbling oneself in a true spirit-state of contrition, in the presence of another human being. This act can be viewed as a giving up of one's ego-self for the benefit of the spirit-self that, in reality, has been transgressed against. Any act committed against self or others that is contrary to the true nature of the God-spirit of love and peace within is the opposite of a life-giving act. That which is not life-giving severs all ties with the spirit that God has placed within all of us.

Such a humbling act as confessing to another human being "the exact nature of our wrongs" is an act that frees our spirit to its natural state of sweetness and innocence.

The Need to Forgive on a Physiological Level

In Chapter III we've talked about how denial causes blocking of energy to all parts of our body. You read that:

1. When you are in denial about your true feelings, you are blocking your true feelings.

2. According to the ancient Chinese art of acupuncture, blocked feelings cause a breakdown in our nervous system.

3. In eastern medicine, the body is said to have many different channels or meridians. Blockage to any of these

meridians causes energy to become restricted, instead of flowing freely into our bodies.

4. It is a known fact, in the eastern culture and in parts of our western culture, that NEGATIVE EMOTIONS DEPRESS THE IMMUNE SYSTEM.

5. Positive thinking allows energy to flow freely throughout our bodies. Meridians are not blocked and we stay healthy, both mentally and physically.

Now, let's get a little more involved with this discussion:

The brain is responsible for receiving and interpreting the information contained within the impulses that the central nervous system creates and transmits to the brain when we see, hear, smell, or touch something. Our eyes could not see without our brain interpreting visual impulses first. We would not be able to hear or understand words being spoken to us, if our brains did not first interpret the auditory impulses of language and noise for us. We would not know that an apple pie, fresh from the oven, smells wonderful or that a warm towel, fresh from the dryer, feels good against our skin after a shower if our brains did not interpret the impulses created by scent and touch for us.

Negative thinking *blocks* impulses from being properly transmitted between the central nervous system and the brain. When this happens, there are a number of consequences as a result. Your brain cannot interpret impulses correctly, and this affects the functioning of your brain and body. You will experience trouble with comprehension of the stimuli around you (people and things). You will find it harder to remember things, resulting in missed appointments and misunderstandings with others. The hormones that act as a *conduit* between the cells of the organs in the body, the central and immune systems and the brain, will not be at the level that the body needs in order to function. This leads to fatigue, sleep disturbances, emotional upsets, physical complaints, and a susceptibility to colds and flu.

When we carry a grudge against a person for an act of transgression against us, any of the thoughts we have about that person or concerning the deed they committed, is more than likely going to be a negative thought. Feelings of anger, guilt, fear, loneliness, shame, and pain will outweigh any feelings of love, joy and passion you may have felt for the person.

From the standpoint of negative emotions depressing the immune system, we can see why it would be to our own advantage to forgive our transgressor, rather than continuing to allow our energies to be drained. In this sense, we are saying that the act of forgiveness allows us to take back our power.

The Need to Forgive on an Emotional Level

Understanding Connection between Personal Strategy for Remembering and Personal Strategy for Forgiving

As I learned more about NLP, I reasoned that the memory strategy we use (either sight, sound or feeling) to remember something from the past is the same strategy we use for forgiving the past. Therefore, knowing a person's personal strategy for remembering the past can assist them in knowing how best to forgive whoever had wronged them. Consequently, **I found the secret to forgiving people in our lives:** it involves finding out how you remember things, based on your own personal strategy. Everyone does it differently, and you'll find out through the experiential exercises that I've scripted, what works best for you.

Below is the reason I believe the same personal strategy we each use for remembering will also help us release and forgive:

In order to forgive, you first have to remember. We've talked about the fact that you cannot work on your issues unless you first break the denial that there is anything wrong. Similarly, you cannot forgive someone unless you first remember that they have done something to you. In the "Refrigerator game," you learned your personal strategy for remembering. As an

Chapter VII. Your Personal Strategy for Forgiving

example, let's say your personal strategy for remembering is visual to kinesthetic to auditory. If it is the V-K-A strategy that makes you remember the transgression done to you, then there is going to be a negative emotion attached to those primary sensory systems—in this case first to your visual sensory system, then to your kinesthetic sensory system, and then to your auditory sensory system, in that order.

Naturally, you must call to mind the transgression in order to deal with it. In doing so, you will quite naturally examine through whatever sensory venue you were most impacted. For instance—was it something that you witnessed your transgressor doing to you (visual)? Or, was it basically what they said to you that hurt the most (auditory)? Or, was it the feeling that you experienced based on what had occurred that brought you the most pain (kinesthetic)? More than likely, the sensory venues that were most impacted by the transgression will be the same as the strategy for remembering. But, let's say that you find that the two are different. Let's say that, even though your strategy for remembering this transgression is V-K-A, you find that the way in which you were most impacted was K-A-V (meaning that you felt violated most by what you felt at the time, followed by something that your transgressor said, followed by something that you saw being done to you).

In order to heal the negative emotions attached to these sensory systems, autogenic exercises (guided imagery) could be implemented, using sensory language delivered in the same order in which the sensory system was damaged. (In this case, visual to kinesthetic to auditory). If, as in our example, there are two strategies in operation that were subsequently damaged, (the one used to remember the transgression and the sensory modes that were most impacted during the transgression) a second autogenic exercise could be employed, using the second sensory mode strategy. This process is a very effective intervention. In fact, very shortly I will give you those experiential exercises I promised that will accomplish this.

FINDING YOUR PERSONAL STRATEGY FOR FORGIVING

Let's start with an example. Pretend that your best friend has said some really awful things about you behind your back. You feel betrayed. You feel that if this person had really been your friend, they wouldn't have said these things in the first place. You feel that you'll never forgive your so-called friend and you're ready to write off the entire friendship. Then your friend calls you and requests a meeting. Somewhat reluctantly you consent to meeting in person to talk out your differences.

The meeting lasts two hours. When you're through, you emerge with your relationship still intact, with a renewed understanding between you. What do you suppose made such a profound difference and changed your initial conviction to forego the friendship?

What did it is a series of internal actions that are dictated by your preferred sensory modes. In other words, you connected to them through your visual, auditory, or kinesthetic modes.

Here's how it's done: I want you to think of an argument that you've had with someone close to you. However, after you talked about it, you both came away with a renewed friendship.

Start by remembering how it went. When you hashed out your grievances, what actually made you shift gears from anger to forgiveness? Was it something that your friend said? Or was it how he or she looked when they said it? Or did you get a gut feeling that they were sincere in their apology to you? It's important that you get an accurate assessment of how things happened. Write down your answer.

After that first response, was there something else that triggered a melting of your heart? Was it how you felt when your friend hugged or held you? Or how their voice sounded as they pledged their future loyalty to you? Or was it something you saw in their eyes? Write down your response to the secondary trigger, that is, the thing that got to you most, after your first response.

Chapter VII. Your Personal Strategy for Forgiving

Next, was there a third interaction that moved you? Was it a visual cue, an auditory cue (something they said or the sound of their voice), or was it kinesthetic (how you felt or a sensation you got either by a physical stimulus such as a hug or kiss, or perhaps a feeling in your gut about it). Write that answer down beside the other two.

Now look at what you've written. If the first response was a response to how they looked—that is Visual. Let's say that after seeing them, the second response that led you to forgive them was to something you heard them say. This is auditory. Finally, you had a good feeling about the entire meeting. You guessed it; kinesthetic. You might want to analyze this one step further and decide what triggered the good feeling. If it was a feeling in response to how they looked, this would be a kinesthetic to visual response. If it was a feeling in response to what you heard them say, this is a kinesthetic to auditory response. Now, I don't want to confuse you, so let's keep it simple. Just jot down your personal strategy for forgiving. Was it Visual-Auditory-Kinesthetic like the above example? What was your answer? You may have found that it was only one or another. Only a visual stimulus? Fine. Only an auditory cue? Maybe it was just the sound of their voice that was enough to melt the icicles hanging from your earlobes. Great. There certainly isn't an answer that is better than the other here. Whatever works for you is perfect!

Now repeat the process. Call to mind or see in your mind's eye another argument that occurred in your life. Ask yourself the same questions in terms of your response. Write these down. How does it compare to the first incident that you recalled? How does this strategy compare with your strategy from the Refrigerator game? What did you find out about your strategy for remembering as compared to your strategy for forgiving?

If you didn't get anything concrete as far as sensory responses, don't be concerned. If you did, remember what your formula was. **This is your personal strategy for forgiving.** This personal formula can be used to unlock a lot of the grudges you've been holding within yourself. This personal formula can become the most life-giving resource you have. You can use it to work toward forgiving anyone you need to in your life.

At this juncture, give yourself some quiet time to reflect on the exercises you've just completed. Reflect on how you came to realize your personal strategy for forgiving. The answers have been locked within all along. Our spirit truly has all the answers!

With this added piece of self-revelation, I want to present to you a set of meditations I've designed as a means of forgiving the people in your life. Use all or one; whichever appeals to your senses. I suggest that you try them all and decide which one gives you the best results. Then, I would continue to focus on that one.

Remember the joke about **Door #1, Door #2,** and **Door #3**? Let's keep the concept of the three doors and change the joke into an exercise for forgiving. (Note: you may record these meditations in your own voice or, for your convenience, a pre-recording of this exercise entitled *Healing through Forgiveness of the Past* is available for purchase. See the last few pages of this book for more information.)

Exercise 1: Door #1

The following is the script for this meditation. Record it the same way you did before. Let your voice guide you in imagery and meditation. Remember to speak slowly and pause where you think it is appropriate to do so.

> Allow yourself to become very comfortable and relaxed. Lie on the floor or in bed or just sit in a comfortable chair. Take some deep breaths, in through your nose, taking your breath all the way past your navel and expel it from your lungs and allow it to leave your body through your mouth. Continue to breathe deeply two or three more times in this manner. Allow your eyelids to relax and feel heavy.

Chapter VII. Your Personal Strategy for Forgiving

As you close your eyes, become aware that your eyes begin to feel as if window blinds are being pulled down over them, as you begin to experience more and more darkness. In this still darkness, begin to imagine your entire body being immersed in a warm fluid. Every muscle of your body is becoming more relaxed as you feel the warm fluid caressing your body, as you sink deeper and deeper into a relaxed state.

Continue to breathe deeply, inhaling through your nose and exhaling through your mouth. (*Pause*) Now, in your mind's eye, notice a door directly in front of you. The door is very thick and heavy. Notice that it is made of oak and is beautifully varnished to a lustrous shine. The door has a golden handle and, as you look at it, a peaceful sensation envelopes you. Feeling secure in doing so, you open the door and walk in.

Look up and realize that you're in the presence of a very majestic entity. An essence of peace and tranquility surrounds this entity, this Divine Being. Perhaps this entity represents God to you. Perhaps it is God for you. What does He look like? Is He fair-skinned or does He have olive or black skin? What does His hair look like? What color is His hair? Can you picture His eyes? What do they look like? See Him looking at you and opening His mouth as if to direct some words to you. You hear Him start to speak to you and you listen intently. Can you hear Him speaking to you? What does his voice sound like? What is this divine entity saying to you? As you hear Him speak to you, become aware of your feelings of being in the presence of God or this god-like being. What are these feelings? Perhaps you can identify fear, hope, anger, guilt, love, passion, or joy. Allow yourself to let these feelings surface. Stay with these feelings.

(I'm going to refer to this entity as God throughout the rest of this exercise.)

Notice now that God is directing your attention to a comfortable chair and inviting you to sit in the chair. God is telling you now to invite another person into the room. He asks you to choose the first person who comes to your mind with whom you have unfinished business. If you feel comfortable in doing so, allow any person who needs forgiving in your life to enter the room and sit in the empty chair that is next to your chair.

Look at your transgressor. Look into their eyes and become aware of what you see there. Become aware of your feelings. Continue to breathe. God asks you to face one another. He asks you to tell this person facing you what they did to you. Speak slowly and clearly. Here is your opportunity to tell this person how you are feeling. (*Pause.*)

Now tell the person how they looked to you when they did what hurt you. If it frightened you, tell them. (*Pause.*) Tell them how they sounded to you when they spoke to you. Tell them what they said to you and describe how you felt when you heard it. (*Pause.*) Tell them what feelings you felt when it happened. (*Pause.*)

And now, listen as the person responds to you. Give them the opportunity to tell you whatever it is that you feel they want to say. Pay attention to the language they use when they talk to you. Do they talk in feeling terms? Are they sincere? Look into their eyes. Listen to the sound of their voice. (*Pause.*) God asks you to tell the person how this incident has affected your life. Tell the person. Remember to be aware of your breathing. (*Pause.*)

God turns to your transgressor. He tells that person to look into your eyes. He asks them if they can see the hurt there. Let the transgressor answer. (*Pause.*) God asks them if they can hear the hurt in your voice. (*Pause.*) He asks them if they can feel the devastation you are feeling. Listen and be open to what your transgressor may say to you. (*Pause.*) God tells you both to go in peace just as you are. He tells you both that He loves you just as you are and that you both have hearts that beat as His own. He tells you to go now in peace.

See yourself getting up from the chair as you very slowly begin to walk to the closed door. It is very important that you are the first to leave the room. See yourself opening the door very slowly. You may look back if you wish. Go in peace. Be careful to shield your eyes from the light of day. Become aware of your breathing. Look around and become aware of the time of day. Be aware of the objects around the room you are in now, in present time, as you become aware of the here and now. Wiggle your fingers and toes and very slowly stretch your body. When you are ready to do so, open your eyes.

I suggest that you give yourself plenty of time to process whatever transpired between yourself and your transgressor. It might take a while to digest everything. Healing takes energy. But, just as aerobic exercise strengthens the heart and increases stamina, so too do spiritual exercises heal and strengthen the heart.

As you process the healing you have accomplished for yourself, remember to breathe. Allow yourself to breathe. Allow yourself to relax. Be gentle with yourself and have respect for your tender humanity. Know that you are a fragile, sacred being who has been violated in many ways in your lifetime. In your soul there is one strong, steady light shining. Be aware that the light will heal and refresh.

In processing, call to mind some of the words you used to talk to your transgressor. Do you recall where the wounds are the deepest? Is it more devastating to look into your transgressor's eyes or to hear his or her voice? Or, maybe the sense of their presence makes the biggest impact on you. Do you feel like you've made headway with forgiving this person? If so, think back to what actually melted your heart. Was it what they said to you, (auditory) or the way they had looked before, during, and/or after they said what they said, (visual) or was it a feeling you got that told you they were really sincere? Remember what you discover because when you decide to work on forgiving someone, this will be of great importance. It gives you insight into the most dominant sensory system that you use when you forgive people. Then you can use the meditations found later in this chapter that are focused specifically for that particular sensory system.

As you process in the next few days or weeks, (don't rush yourself; let it happen as it happens) it will be extremely beneficial for you to journal. Write down the responses that you gave your transgressor and that he or she gave you. This interaction is useful to record. It will help to get the feelings out of your body (remember our Sensory Escape exercise). If you have a person in your life who you feel can be trusted, you might decide to read the dialogue out loud to them. This will especially impact you if you happen to be an auditory person or at least operating in your auditory mode as part of your strategy for forgiving.

In the next few weeks, you may want to try the entire exercise again. Listen to the recording you made. Breathe. You may get a few more pieces of the puzzle. Always give yourself processing time because you need to guard against emotional overload.

Explore the feelings you experienced during the exercise and any feelings that come up during your processing and journaling. Write them all down. Stand in front of the mirror and say them. Say "I feel lonely." "I feel angry." (Or whatever you are feeling). Look at what your face is doing as you speak. What do you observe? Tight muscles at the corners of your mouth? Hear the sound of your voice. What does it sound like? Pay attention to how you're feeling as you look at your face and hear your voice saying how you're feeling. It'll also help to go back to the Sensory Escape exercise. If you haven't yet recorded it, do so now. Play this back for yourself, so that you can get rid of any negative feelings that have surfaced during the exercise.

When you have given yourself ample time (days or weeks) to process all that has surfaced, you may decide to tackle what you'll find behind **Door #2.**

Exercise 2: Door #2

(After looking over this exercise so that you know where you're headed, put it on your recording device so that you may then play it back and take the suggestions of your own voice.)

Chapter VII. Your Personal Strategy for Forgiving

Close your eyes and get comfortable. Start your breathing exercises. Inhale through your nose and exhale through your mouth. (*Pause*) Again, inhale through your nose, this time taking it all the way down past your navel. Really expand your rib cage. Exhale through your mouth. Pay attention to any tension anywhere in your body and direct the flow of breathing toward that tension. Continue to breathe and direct healing energy toward any tension in your body.

When you are relaxed enough to do so, become aware of a bright red door in front of you. See yourself going toward this door. Hear your footsteps getting louder and quicker as you become eager to see and experience and sense what is behind the door. Open the door little by little and peek in. There you see all the people in your life who need forgiving for something they've done to you. You also see all the people in your life with whom you need to ask forgiveness. (*Long pause.*)

Go to each one, one at a time. If you can, maintain eye contact with each one of them. (*Pause.*) As you go to each one of them, hear their voices. (*Pause.*) Feel their presence. (*Pause.*) What do you feel as you experience each of these people? Anger? Hatred? What would you like to say to them? (*Pause.*) How do they look as you are saying it? (*Pause.*)

It will be helpful now for everyone in the room to form a circle. All the people in your life who need to forgive or be forgiven have come into the circle with you. Look at the faces of each of these people, one by one. (*Pause.*) As you look at these people, notice that everyone is bound together at the wrist with heavy chains and that each chain is linked to the next person. Realize that all the chains lead back to you. Feel the weight of the chains. Do they feel heavy?

Become aware of two white doves in the room. Watch as these doves of peace circle everyone. Watch as the doves begin loosening and unraveling all the chains. The chains that bind you to one another are loosened and all of you are set free. Really feel the difference; take the time to experience the difference. Do you feel lighter than you did with all those chains weighing you down? (*Pause for a short time.*)

Willingly extend your hand to the person sitting next to you in the circle. Allow that person, in turn, to extend his or her hand to the person sitting next to them. Watch as each person reaches out to the person next to them, until all of you are connected. (*Pause.*) Become aware of a very exhilarating white light that begins to penetrate the top of your head. (*Pause.*) Continue to breathe. Allow the white light to travel through your head, onto the back of your neck, traveling down through the arm you've extended to the person on your right. Watch as the warm beam of white light travels from your hand to the hand of the person to your right. Feel the sensation. Be aware of the light as it travels up their hand, through their arm, straight through their body, out their other arm, and is transported to the person next to them. (*Pause.*)

Watch this process continue until all are connected by this warm, all-encompassing light. (*Pause.*)

Stand in silence and become aware of the sound of a heartbeat. (*Pause.*) A sound of a single heartbeat, that at first is a faint sound, and as you stand connected, each in the other's energy, you are aware of the faint sound becoming stronger and stronger, louder and louder. Feel a deep sense of God's peace over all of you. Stand there for a few more moments. (*Pause.*) When you are ready, quietly leave the circle and leave the room. You may look back if you want to. Remember to shield your eyes from the light of day as you close the door to the room behind you. You are facing a brand-new wonderful day on the other side of the door you just closed. Open your eyes to this bright new day.

The only way out of the pain from our childhood traumas, whether instigated within the religious school system or elsewhere, is to walk through the pain. With that thought in mind, let me give you another meditation (or sensory exercise). With all this work you're doing, I'll again suggest that you talk to a professional therapist. It's very rare that such heavy-duty work can be dealt with alone.

CHAPTER VII. YOUR PERSONAL STRATEGY FOR FORGIVING

After the exercise I've just presented to you, I suggest that you allow enough process time; journal and do the feeling exercise in front of a mirror. When you're ready to enter Door #3, you'll know. Remember to read it through before you record it so you'll know what to expect. Then, read it into a recording device. Afterwards, play it back so you may experience it.

Exercise 3: Door #3

Become aware of your breathing. (*Pause about 20 seconds.*) Allow any tension to escape every time you breathe out your mouth. Continue to breathe deeply as you get rid of any tension in your body. When you feel relaxed enough, begin to recall the people from the Door #2 exercise with whom you were bound. Select one of these people. (*Pause and give yourself time to make the decision.*)

And now, enter Door #3 with the person you've chosen. As the two of you enter, become aware of another presence in the room. A peace envelopes you, as you discover that the other presence is God or a divine entity. He directs you and the other person to sit in two chairs, facing each other. You instinctively know He will lovingly guide you both to a deeper understanding and forgiving.

Sit in one of the chairs, facing the other person. Watch as the other person walks to the remaining chair. Picture he or she speaking slowly and clearly, as they look straight at you and say, "I ask forgiveness for what I've done to you." (*Pause.*) Feel their presence. (*Pause.*) Hear their voice. (*Pause.*) Look into their eyes. What do you see? (*Pause.*) If you are ready to do so, then respond: "I forgive you." (*Pause.*) There may be another transgression they committed against you. If so, listen as they ask your forgiveness. (*Pause.*) In like manner, they continue with any other transgressions they have committed against you. In response to each, merely say, "I forgive you" if you are ready to do so. (*Pause for 30 seconds when you are recording this.*)

And now, is there anything you did to this person that you want them to forgive? (*Pause.*) If so, mention the transgression and ask forgiveness. Listen as he or she responds to you. (*Pause.*) Feel their presence. If you can, look into their eyes. Continue this until nothing is left unsaid. (*Pause.*) Before you end your time together, is there anything else you want to say to this person? (*Pause.*) Listen to hear if there is anything else they have left unsaid. (*Pause.*)

When both of you have finished, get out of your chair. Decide in which manner you will leave the room. Perhaps you will want to leave the room first. Perhaps you have made the decision to allow the *other* person to exit the room first. Maybe you've decided that it is appropriate for you both to leave the room together. Whatever decision you have made, do it now. As you prepare to leave, again be aware of God's loving presence.

Feel enveloped in peace and love and the eternal presence of God. Smile and be content with the knowledge that you will always be guided by God. All that is necessary is to ask. Take a deep breath full of serenity and forgiveness, allowing it to fill your being and let you relax. Slowly advance toward the door now and step into the bright daylight sun. It is very important to not look back, only forward. You may want to shield your eyes from the sun and brightness of the brand new day.

Now that you've experienced these forgiveness techniques in visual, auditory, and kinesthetic rituals, you've probably learned which sensory language works best for you. If the visuals worked best for you, (looking at the person or maintaining eye contact) remember that. Maybe the auditory cues—listening to the sound of their voice, hearing your own voice—worked best for you. Or maybe the kinesthetic (feeling) cues work best. With this knowledge, you can choose to concentrate your energies on the areas that work best for you.

Healing is a life-long process. If you're on the chosen avenue of spiritual awakening, you've elected to deal with your pain;

really face your spiritual fires. As long as you and I are living, we will encounter hurts along the way. If we choose to handle the pain in a healthy way and do the work necessary, we will heal. Some may choose to handle the pain in a self-destructive way, stuffing down the pain with food; numbing the pain with alcohol; medicating the pain with drugs; dulling the senses with overwork. The healing work gets less painful as we go. We only do as much as we can handle without getting overloaded. So, you may have to take one transgressor at a time. Is it hard work? You bet it is. But in the end you'll be rewarded by a higher spiritual understanding.

As was the case in the exercises you did prior to this one, it's necessary to give yourself several days before you pursue this further. You don't want emotional overload. You can burn out on self-help techniques, as with anything else. You know what they say about having too much of a good thing. Some of you may be shaking your head in exasperation over that one. You may be asking: "If it's supposed to be so good for me, why do I feel so sad or depressed?" Remember, in order to heal, you must first walk through the pain.

I'm reminded of a one inch cut on my hand that I received many years ago, as a result of a misguided paring knife. A few hours after I had accidently delivered this wound to myself, it looked and felt pretty good. I had managed to stop the bleeding with the application of many cotton swabs, I could see the skin underneath, and I anticipated a speedy healing. What I'd overlooked was the next step in the healing process, which was a complete opening of the wound. It looked very unattractive, but I knew that it was healing. I don't have to take you step by step through this analogy, but it reminds us all of the way the human heart and psyche work. As unattractive as it sounds, looks and feels, sometimes we have to tolerate unattractive wounds before we begin to grow and heal.

Of course, that's just what happened to my hand wound. It began closing and scarring over until finally, not even the scar was visible. Now, I'm not trying to dilute the process. Some scars, as you probably already know, never completely go away. But you get measures of healing, regardless. THE ONLY WAY OUT IS THROUGH! And, as I tell my patients and clients, TRUST THE PROCESS!

Chapter VII. Your Personal Strategy for Forgiving

Things to Remember After Reading Chapter VII:

- Making peace with someone who has done something to you heals YOUR soul.

- Forgiveness is something we do for OURSELVES.

- Forgiving someone does not mean we will allow them to hurt us again. It does not mean what they did was OK. It means we honor ourselves enough to let go of the feelings of anger.

- Anger holds our Spirit for ransom; forgiveness frees our Spirit.

Chapter VII Affirmation:

"I let go of my past so that I may walk forward into my future."

Epilogue

God's Pure Child: Back to the Innocence

Epilogue
God's Pure Child: Back to the Innocence

The best way to conclude our time together is to become aware of your feelings right now. You may have made quantum leaps while reading this book and doing some of the experiential exercises. Maybe you're feeling like you haven't made any headway at all. I guarantee that if you've come this far with me, you <u>have</u> made tremendous progress, although you might not be aware of it yet. Sometimes it takes several days or weeks to process an entirely new perception or mindset. Maybe you're feeling raw inside from all the feelings that have surfaced. Keep in mind that feelings are neither good nor bad; they are just our feelings that need to be expressed in a healthy way!

Sometimes when we're in the middle of a crisis or a discomfort, we cannot see, hear or feel the end of it. Remember that there's a natural progression of things. Sometimes we fail to look at the larger scope of things. Do you recall the yearning we talked about in Chapter IV? If there's something that you're yearning for so badly you can taste it, remember that you already have it. Maybe you're starting to make the connection in your heart with what forgiveness can bring you. Maybe you've realized that it can and will bring you back to the sweetness of your innocent youth.

I remember that for years I felt bitter, hard and old inside. I was in my early thirties and really felt bogged down. I was reminded of this just the other day when a friend and I were looking through photographs of that period of my life. He remarked that my body had been in tip-top condition, but my face looked very hard. Now, at sixty-five, I feel vibrant and alive! The difference—forgiveness! Over thirty years later, I have a real zest for life! Everyday I feel a joy in my soul that I very often cannot contain! I enjoy filling the entire house with laughter. Last year, another friend asked a relative of mine if I'd had a face lift! The only thing that has lifted from me is the hardness!

Ironically enough, my body had to get very, very ill before my spirit could soar! While returning to good health I learned that where there is a health problem, there is a forgiveness problem.

You're standing on the horizon of your life right now. Look out as far as your eyes can see. You can create in your heart everything that your eyes see for your future. Hear the sounds of your life—the past, the present. Know that you can create the sounds of your future.

Feel the sensations in your heart right now. Remember the sensations in your past. Remember how they bogged you down. Know that you can create honey-sweet sensations for yourself today for the future.

Before I got very ill, I defined success by the amount of hard work I did and by my life accomplishments. The busier I was, the more successful. Or so I thought. Suddenly, I could do nothing but lie in bed all day. I learned that I had to re-define success for myself. Today, success for me isn't what I do, how much I do, how much money I make or what kind of car I drive. It isn't the house in which I live or the clothes I wear. For me, success is measured by the energy created as a soul reaches out to assist another soul. Success for me, today, is that I've come back to God—the Sweetness, the Light. And I've learned to forgive in my life.

I believe I've also re-defined the concepts of Heaven and Hell for myself. Today, my concept of Hell on earth is being entrenched in bitterness, hatred, and jealousy. Beyond that, I have no fear of the threats of eternal damnation that were always lurking in my mind as a child. I know that I have a loving Father in Heaven who isn't waiting to zap me to Hell the first chance He has. The punitive God of my youth is gone.

Epilogue: God's Pure Child: Back to the Innocence

I cannot imagine what Heaven is like. Few people can—we have such a limited scope as human beings here on earth. But I sense it when I hug my son Ron, and feel his strength and courage; I get a glimmer of it as I look into my beautiful daughter Marianna's green eyes; I hear it when my grandson Scotty boy runs to me and says, "Grandma, I love you." I feel it when my little granddaughter Erica clings to me as I sing her to sleep with *You Are My Special Angel.* We're all Heaven to each other here on earth. We are Christ for one another.

In 1984, when I invited God into my life again, it started the biggest adventure I've ever known! He has done things for me that I could never do on my own. All it takes is a willingness to let go of having to be in control at all times. When I let go of having to do it on my own, all the doors opened up!

The really satisfying and carefree thing about turning everything over to God is that you always know that when He is in charge of your life, you're always where you're supposed to be. Even in bad times. With pain there is growth, even though while we are in the pain we sometimes cannot see the good. There are always blessings and lessons that come out of the adversity in our lives.

God is not a Catholic, nor is He Baptist, Lutheran, Presbyterian, Methodist, or any other denomination. God is non-denominational. He isn't concerned with all the man-made dogma and rules. He *is* concerned with how we love our brothers, sisters, and ourselves and how we serve Him. He has His eye on us and He loves us, just the way we are. If the Divine maker of Heaven and earth loves us just the way we are, we must all be very special! Live your life that way.

May God bless you with the yearnings of your heart!

Chapter by Chapter Outline

Part I: Organizing Our Inner Resources

I. Why Sister Mary Discipline Can't Get You Anymore

    Nunsense!

    Forgiveness as a Tool for Healing

II. Establishing Our Goals

    Eleanor's Story

    Innocence and Sweetness

    Neurolinguistic Programming: What it is and How it Can Help You Forgive

        NLP as a Modality for Remembering

        Using NLP to Help Heal Memories

        Using NLP as a Modality for Forgiveness

    Why Forgive?

    Things to Remember After Reading Chapter II

    Chapter Affirmation

III. Breaking the Denial

    Three Steps to Breaking Denial

        Step I: Journaling

        Step II: Sharing Your Journal

        Step III: Hearing Others Tell Their Stories

            Joseph's Story

            Ben's Story

The Case of Father Porter

Unthawing Your Feelings

Things to Remember After Reading Chapter III

Chapter Affirmation

IV. Awareness and Yearning as Resources for Healing

Awareness as a Resource for Healing

Physical Abuse

Kenneth's Story

Sexual Abuse

Jonathan's Story

Intellectual Abuse

Elaine's Story

Emotional Abuse

Arthur's Story

Spiritual Abuse

Rebecca's Story

Betty's Story

Yearning as a Resource for Healing

Things to Remember After Reading Chapter IV

Chapter Affirmation

V. Understanding as a Resource for Healing

Dealing With Abandonment: Why Did They Change All the Rules?

Rules that Were Changed

Feedback from Catholics Concerning the Changes

- Some Catholics Lost Trust in the Church
- Feelings of Abandonment Reported
- People Resist Change
- Changes Meant Freedom to Many
- Knowledge of Personality Type Can Help Heal
  - Melancholy Temperament
  - Take the Four Temperament Personality Indicator
  - Results of Phase II of the Study
- Knowledge of Your Preferred Sensory Mode Can Help Heal
- Vulnerability of the Kinesthetic Sensory Mode
- Healing from Deep Traumatic Abuse
- Obsessive-Compulsive Disorder
  - Breeding Ground for OCD
  - Blame vs. Taking Responsibility
- Shame-Based Society
  - Schools Set-Up for Toxic Shame
  - Sexual Abuse among Religious Leaders
  - Religion Addicts
  - Sex Addicts
  - Cross-Addiction: Religion Addicts/Sex Addiction
  - Physical and Sexual Abuse Survivors
- Things to Remember After Reading Chapter V
- Chapter Affirmation

VI. You're Too Old to Play Victim Anymore: Formula for Getting Rid of Victim Thinking

The Refrigerator Game

Looking at Our Inner Resources

    Inner Resources for Healing Trauma

    The "Poop" Joke

Formula for Stamping Out Victim Thinking

    1. Be aware of Victim Sentences

    2. Breathe

    3. Sensory Stop and Take Charge Exercise

    4. Sentence Reversal

    5. Sensory Affirmation Exercise

    6. Sensory Escape Exercise

    7. Sensory Journaling Exercise

Here is the Experiential Part of Our Formula

Wrapping It Up

Things to Remember After Reading Chapter VI

Chapter Affirmation

Part II: Healing Through Forgiveness of the Past

VII. Your Personal Strategy for Forgiving: What to do with the Feelings

    Why Forgive?

        Need to Forgive on a Spiritual Level

        Need to Forgive on a Physiological Level

        Need to Forgive on an Emotional Level

    Finding Your Personal Strategy for Forgiving

        Exercise 1: Door #1

        Exercise 2: Door #2

        Exercise 3: Door #3

    Things to Remember After Reading Chapter VII

    Chapter Affirmation

VIII. Epilogue: Back to the Innocence

Appendix I

To All Adults Who Were Enrolled in a Religious School System at the Primary or High School Level:

This questionnaire is part of an independent study on the effects, either productive or adverse, of being educated in a religious school system of any denomination, (e.g. Catholic, Jewish, Lutheran). The information derived from this study will be used in a manuscript I am researching and preparing entitled:

God Is Not a Catholic:
A Recovery Journey for Adult Children of Parochial Schools

Despite what the title may suggest to you, the manuscript is NOT a slur against the Catholic religion (or any religion for that matter). The title merely refers to the fact that we have a loving God who doesn't take issue with the denomination that we choose to use as a vehicle to travel back to Him.

The focus of the book is a move toward forgiveness. This is your opportunity to be heard, whether you've always felt that you had been treated adversely in your school system or whether you've always felt that the media hasn't given the religious school system a fair shake.

Your participation in this endeavor will be greatly appreciated. All information that you give will be treated with absolute confidentiality. As you'll note, there's a space for your first name only. Please do not sign your name at all, unless you are consenting to a possible interview. In this case, sign only your first name, and fill in your area code and phone number so that I may contact you. Fill in the space for your address only if you would like a return reply with results of this study and publication information. In this case, you're asked to include a self-addressed stamped envelope with this questionnaire so that I can mail this information to you. Replies of this nature will be mailed after March 1, 1993 but no later than May 3, 1997. (You may address the envelope to yourself as *Questionnaire Participant* instead of your name.)

Questions pertaining to your gender, religious affiliation, state in which you lived at the time, and period attended will be used for demographic purposes only. I may choose to use any information in lectures or seminars; this will be done anonymously.

Thank you in advance for your willingness to be a part of this study. Feel free to make copies and pass this on to anyone who qualifies by having had gone to a religious school.

APPENDICES

Independent Study Questionnaire

© D.M. Pela 1992

Aug. 1, 1992-Feb. 1, 1997

1. Sex __M__F

2. Religious affiliation of school you attended (Catholic, Lutheran, Jewish, etc.)

   _____

3. Name of state in which school was located

   _____

4. What age(s) were you?_____

5. Grades you attended_____

6. I attended religious school in the (check one):

   1940's_____   late 40's-early 50's_____

   1950's_____   late 50's-early 60's_____

   1960's_____   late 60's-early 70's_____

   1970's_____

7. Were your school days in this facility (check as many as apply):

   happy_____   sad_____   painful_____

   still carry happy memories_____

still carry painful scars_____

don't remember most of it_____

enjoy talking about it_____

don't enjoy talking about it_____

would rather forget about it____

still an issue in my life_____

not an issue in my life_____

I attribute the many good values and morals which I possess today to my religious school training_____

I feel that much of my thinking today is tainted by guilt, shame and fear which I feel were used as teaching tools._____

I am working through some issues in my life that I feel are related to this._____

I am working through some issues in my life that I feel are a direct result of my years in this school._____

I don't feel like I'm working through anything but feel it's something I should address at some point in my life._____

I feel that I have nothing to work through, as I'm completely satisfied with that particular school system._____

8. Do you feel that guilt was incorporated as a teaching tool? _____ (if yes, answer a. through d.)

   a. Define guilt.

   _____

   _____

b. What was the focus of the guilt? (e.g. "if you do this, you'll go to Hell").

_____

_____

_____

c. Do you feel guilt-ridden as an adult? Y   N

d. If so, do you attribute it to your religious school days? Y   N

9 Do you feel you were shamed by the teachers? Y   N
(if yes, answer a. through d.)

a. Define shame

_____

_____

_____

b. In retrospect, how did the shame manifest itself? (feelings of inferiority or being defective.)

_____

_____

_____

c. Do you feel "shame based" as an adult? Y   N

d. If yes, do you attribute it to your school training? Y   N

10 Do you feel that fear was used as a teaching tool? Y   N
(if yes, answer a. through c.)

   a. How?

   b. Would you describe yourself as a fearful person?_____

   c. If so, do you attribute some of that fear to your religious school training? _____

11 In retrospect, would you say that you were ever tormented by a case of scruples? (thinking everything you did was very wrong and because of doing it, you were sure to go to Hell)? Y   N

   a. Was there an incident that initiated these scruples?
   Y   N

   b. If so, what was it?

   _____
   _____
   _____
   _____

   IF YOU REQUIRE MORE SPACE FOR ANY OF YOUR ANSWERS, YOU MAY USE NOTEBOOK PAPER.

12. What effect, if any, do you feel your religious school background had on your present relationship with, or lack of relationship with, God?

   _____
   _____
   _____
   _____

13. What effect, if any, do you feel your religious school background had on your present attitudes toward sex?

_____

_____

_____

14 a. Do you feel or have you ever felt that you at times exhibit obsessive-compulsive behavior? Y   N

   b. Define obsessive-compulsive behavior:

   _____

   _____

   _____

Because the Catholic religion alone had the mortal sin/venial sin rule and the use of the confessional, question 15 only applies to people who have gone through Catholic school. All others may go on to question 16.

15. Did you find yourself afraid of confession? Y   N

    As part of your scruples, were you too hard on yourself, thinking everything you did was a sin?

    Subsequently, were you afraid and ashamed to tell these "sins," left them out and thought you'd made a "bad confession?" Y   N

    Did this trigger a pattern of torment and anguish because of a stockpile of "bad confessions" and "bad communions?" Y   N

    If you can relate to this, would you care to share similar experiences? Please do so on notebook paper.

16. If the absolute worst violation was done to you—a sexual molestation—and you'd like to write about it, you may use any or all of the space on the backs of these sheets.

Thank you for your time and co-operation. You've just taken part in a universal healing. Information compiled will also be used in my seminars on *Healing through Forgiveness of the Past* and a concurrent transcript. The objective is not to cast stones. I believe the religious leaders of the world did and are doing the best they know how to do. I believe the time is right for a universal healing through forgiving our transgressors. In order to do this, the silence must first be broken.

Check one:

_____ I consent to an interview.

First name only _____
Phone no.(_____)_____
_____I do not want an interview
_____I am enclosing a self-addressed stamped envelope. I'd like to be sent the results of this study and publication information on the book.
Return completed questionnaire to:
Dianne Pela
Center for Emotional & Spiritual Empowerment
3115 W. Mountain View Rd. Ste. A-224
Phoenix, AZ. 85051   Phone: 480-266-9546

Appendix II

Results of Questionnaire

People who had attended a parochial school in the 1940's through the 1960's, at either the elementary or high school level, were asked to fill out these questionnaires. 1500 questionnaires were circulated. These figures are based on the 1000 people who returned a completed questionnaire and/or gave me an interview. This study was conducted in the states of Ohio, Michigan, Arizona and California. Because people move away from their state of origin after they've attended school there, the states represented are Ohio, Michigan, Arizona, California, Pennsylvania, Montana, North Dakota, Florida, and Georgia. In essence, what was intended to be a random sampling of states, turned out to be a small sampling of western, eastern and southern states.

58% of the participants were female; 42% were male.

Because of the even distribution here, gender is not a variable.

68 (7%) attended both a religious grade school and high school.

30 (3%) attended only a religious high school.

902 (90%) attended only primary grades K-8 in a religious school.

(Of these, only 32 had some kind of combination from public to parochial school.)

129 (13%) attended in 1940's.

153 (14%) attended in late 1940's-early 1950's.

157 (16%) attended in 1950's.

125 (13%) attended in late 1950's-early 1960's.

139 (14%) attended in 1960's.

142 (14%) attended in late 1960's-early 1970's.

155 (16%) attended grade school in 1970's.

There was a very even distribution of generation.

760 (76%) of all the participants said they had sad, painful memories and don't enjoy talking about it.

780 (78%) said they attributed their good morals and values to their experience in the religious school system. As you will see, this figure correlates directly with the percentage of people who were molested by a member of the clergy, who gave a definite "no" to this.

910 (91%) said much of their thinking today is guilt ridden, shame filled, and fearful. They said they believe that guilt, fear and shame were used as teaching tools or to manipulate a certain kind of behavior. What these last two figures tell us is that many people, although of the opinion that the religious school system had laid a firm foundation of good values and morals, still recognize that guilt, shame and fear were used to manipulate.

382 (38%) people said they were working through issues today that they believe are related to their experience in the religious school system. (This, to me, is sad because it reflects that half the people who reported having had painful scars, are not working through their issues.)

820 (82%) people said they feel guilt-ridden as an adult. Of these, 782 (78%) attributed this to their upbringing in the religious school system.

890 (89%) said they feel shame-based as an adult. All attributed it to their religious school days.

382 (38%) said they would describe themselves as a fearful person today. Of the 187 people interviewed, 50% said they attribute this to a combination of both parental and school influence.

380 (38%) said they had suffered a severe case of scruples as a child.

680 (68%) said they felt they had a good relationship with God today because of their experiences in school.

200 (20%) said they had a bad or tainted relationship with God because of their experience in school.

120 (12%) people said their schooling had no influence on their present relationship with God.

170 (17%) said their healthy attitude toward sex today was a direct result of their religious schooling.

220 (22%) said their unhealthy or adverse attitudes toward sex were derived from their schooling.

610 (61%) people said their schooling had nothing to do with their present attitudes on sex, either way.

Let's look at some of the random answers to the questions in the study. I've combined the questions, "What was the focus of the guilt?", "How did the shame manifest itself?", and "What were some incidents triggering the scruples?" And some of the answers were:

1. "The inference that I'm bad and anything I do to be good is hopeless."
2. "The nuns would tell us frightening stories about people who were on their way to confession only to get into a car

accident and die. Because they had been unconscious and not able to make the 'Act of Contrition' they were damned to Hell. The 'mortal sins' were still on their souls."

3. "Rather than instill motivation in children to perform, they used [the threat of] damnation to force results."

4. "I recall the scruples that I had and it was pure hell. But, now I realize that the adult-level scruples that I still can get locked into can be reasoned with." [sic]

5. "A story of cause and effect, which was narrated by a nun, ended up in satanic possession of a child's body."

Here are samples of the answers to the query about whether their schooling had any influence on their present relationship with God:

1. "I don't bother with any organized religion. I figure it's me and God. That's all. All the other ritualized things don't matter."

2. "I admit that I'm really put off by God. I know that it is about my school days. I also know that God had nothing to do with it. I just feel like an empty shell where God is concerned. It seems too hard to do. I don't even know how I would go about getting a relationship with God now. I know it's a goal in my life, but right now it's on the back burner."

3. "I thank God for my parochial school background. It's because of this excellent training that I have high morals and values. I've shared this with my husband and passed it along to my children."

Out of the 220 people who reported a sexual molestation by either a nun or priest or some other member of clergy, there were only a few who cared to go into it on the questionnaire, or consent to an interview.

Now that you've looked at the figures in the study you may wonder why they all tend to be slanted very heavily against the parochial school system. I believe it may be the types of people involved in the study. By that I mean that many of the people who were receptive to a study of this nature already had an axe to grind. If you were handed a questionnaire related to an issue about which you felt you'd been treated unfairly, you would be more apt to participate than if you were handed a questionnaire concerning an issue that pleased you.

For example, how many people do you think fill out the warranty and information on a new appliance they just purchased? If they are entirely happy with the appliance, rarely do they sit down and write the company. However, let there be cause to gripe about that appliance, and they very quickly write the company with a letter of complaint. This is human nature. I'm saying that people without complaints about the parochial school system opted to stay away from the study. They were the very people who could've made a difference in the statistics that were so slanted.

But, let's not stray from the purpose of this study. It wasn't for condemnation. It was to give credence and awareness to the idea that, as a direct result of being educated in the religious school systems, there are areas in many lives that need healing. Now that we've gotten in touch with our hurts, we can begin the work of healing.

There were many nice things said by people who felt they had had enriching and worthwhile experiences in their schools. One of the more touching tributes to the days spent in a parochial school came from a woman in her late thirties, who resides in Florida now, but had spent her childhood in the midwest. She wrote:

> "In spite of the fear tactics, I always found God to be a loving God who was always there for me. My religious upbringing has brought me closer to Him. I guess I tried to pull more of the positive side of my eight year 'nunhood.' My religion has

been my strength. The 'guilt and shame' thing is merely due to narrow-mindedness of pre-Vatican [Council] teachings. Being in school during the Vatican council changes, I felt doors opening and the face of God changed from scorn to love."

Appendix III

Neurolinguistic Programming
Preferred Sensory Mode Indicator

1. Given a choice, would you rather:
    a. Go to a movie.
    b. Go to a concert and listen to good music.
    c. Get a massage.
2. When you are at a concert, do you:
    a. Watch the musicians as the music plays.
    b. Close your eyes and listen to every note.
    c. Tap your foot or hand to the music.
3. When you go to an amusement park, are you most attracted to:
    a. Rides which are colorful and animated.
    b. Rides that contain musical tunes or that tell a story.
    c. Rides that give you a sensation in the pit of your stomach.
4. When you see a movie, which do you prefer?
    a. Action motion pictures with spectacular views.
    b. Musicals.
    c. Romantic themes where the boy always gets the girl.
5. What would you most like about riding the Ferris wheel?
    a. The view from the top.
    b. Listening to the screams and excitement of the crowd.
    c. The anticipation when going up and the free sensation when going down.

6. If you were asked to memorize a phone number, the most effective way to do that would be:
   a. I would see it in my mind's eye.
   b. I would repeat it over and over again to myself.
   c. I would associate it with something else to make it easy to remember.

7. If you were purchasing a home, what would be the best selling point for you?
   a. The overall look of the place.
   b. The surrounding sounds of the neighborhood.
   c. The feeling you get when you enter each room.

8. Why did you buy your car?
   a. You like the color or the way it looks.
   b. You like the way it sounds—the exhaust system, horn or stereo system.
   c. You like the way it feels to drive, the way it handles on the road, or the speed it is capable of producing.

9. What is the best way to learn math as a child?
   a. Flash cards, charts.
   b. Repeatedly saying patterns, such as times tables, to yourself until they are memorized.
   c. Counting on your fingers or associating the numbers with other things that feel right to you.

10. What best describes what happens when I set a goal for myself:
    a. I like to imagine what I would look like as I attain my goal.
    b. I can hear the praises of friends, family and colleagues.
    c. I feel satisfied that I am aiming toward something.

11. Think of the best friend you ever had. What did you value about that friendship?
    a. The way we viewed ourselves together as friends.
    b. The sound of their voice or the interesting way in which we conversed with one another.
    c. The way we connected emotionally, intellectually, or on a personal level.

12. What do you remember most about your first romantic crush in elementary or high school?
    a. What they looked like.
    b. The sound of their voice.
    c. How it felt to walk hand-in-hand or kiss them.

13. What is the most important thing for you in a relationship?
    a. How we look together or how my partner takes care of how he/she looks.
    b. The quality of our conversations together; what we can say to each other.
    c. Touching, embracing, holding, kissing, walking hand-in-hand.

14. How do you know someone loves you?
    a. They take pictures of me and show them to friends; they like to be seen with me.
    b. They constantly tell me how much they love and care for me.
    c. They put their arms around me and hold me in a very tender, gentle manner.

15. How do you best connect with your love?
    a. I want to see them.
    b. I want to hear their voice.
    c. I want to feel their embrace.

16. My ideal backyard would contain:
    a. Attractive landscaping, bridges, colorful flowers.
    b. Babbling brook, wind-chimes, chirping birds.
    c. Swimming pool, hot tub, hammock.

17. Of these careers, what would interest you the most:
    a. Graphic designer, photographer, fashion designer.
    b. Musician, sound engineer, counselor.
    c. Professional athlete, massage therapist, airplane pilot.

18. At work, it is most important that:
    a. My workspace includes pictures of loved ones on my desk.
    b. I can hear my co-workers around me talking or laughing, or a radio is on in the background.
    c. I have a comfortable chair in which to sit and the lighting is relaxing and soft.

19. What would be your deciding factor when purchasing clothing?
    a. When I try it on and see my reflection in the mirror, I look attractive wearing it.
    b. The salesperson says, "You really look great in that!"
    c. The article of clothing feels cozy and I feel comfortable wearing it.

20. Think of your favorite sport. What do you like most about it?
    a. Watching the sport or enjoying the view.
    b. Listening to the sounds of the team or the crowd.
    c. Being active in the sport. Enjoying the feel of holding the bat or kicking the ball.

21. When you cook, what is most important when it is finished?
    a. How it looks; presentation.
    b. Getting compliments from dinner guests.
    c. How it tastes; flavor.

22. What relaxes you most?
    a. Watching a sunset.
    b. Soft music or a white noise generator.
    c. Sitting in a hot tub.

23. What do you like best about walking on the beach?
    a. Watching the ocean waves as they flow in and out or observing others surfing and swimming.
    b. Hearing the sounds of the sea gulls and the waves crashing onto the shoreline.
    c. Feeling the sand beneath your toes and the warmth of the sun.

24. Choose the type of pet that you would most gravitate toward:
    a. Pets you can observe such as tropical fish, chameleons or tortoises.
    b. Pets you can listen to such as chirping parakeets or talking parrots.
    c. Pets you can cuddle like a cat or a rabbit.

25. When I am feeling fearful about something in my life:
    a. My world looks dark and shattered.
    b. Sounds are very disturbing to me.
    c. I feel off-centered and unbalanced.

Now, add up the three separate scores of A's, B's and C's. The letter with the highest number indicates that this is probably your primary sensory system. (Remember that you will still use all three or a combination of all three sensory modes to perform different tasks throughout the day.)

Appendix IV

The Four Temperaments Indicator: Determining Your Most Dominant Personality Type

Circle the answer that MOST reflects who you are:

1. Typically, most of my thoughts are focused on:
    a. Events that occurred in the past.
    b. Current events in my life.
    c. Goal-oriented toward the future.
    d. I prefer to be uninvolved and am most comfortable as a spectator of my life.

2. My life theme is:
    a. To avoid conflict.
    b. To be perfect.
    c. To be in control at all times.
    d. To have fun and talk to friends a lot.

3. My decisions are based primarily on:
    a. My intuition.
    b. An extensive analysis of the situation.
    c. My feelings concerning the situation.
    d. The solution that would involve the least work and/or conflict.

4. I would be most prone to depression if:
    a. There were several imperfections in my life.
    b. There was not a lot of fun in my life.
    c. My life seemed out of control.
    d. I was forced to face conflict and take a stand.

5. The best stress relievers for me would be:
   a. TV/eating/reading.
   b. Study/meditation/withdrawal
   c. More work/exercise.
   d. Compulsive shopping or eating.

6. My most important emotional needs:
   a. I need to feel productive. I need to be perceived as a good provider and appreciated for my hard work.
   b. I need constant encouragement, love, self-sufficiency, and validation.
   c. I need to be noticed and praised. I need to feel secure.
   d. I need encouragement or gentle prodding.

7. The best description of the weaknesses in my relationships are:
   a. I can be domineering, intimidating and unemotional. Sometimes I have a sharp tongue.
   b. Sometimes I avoid responsibility. I can be selfish and lack motivation.
   c. The imperfections of my mate really bother me. I am too sensitive and easily depressed.
   d. I have not always acted with integrity regarding money or the opposite sex.

8. Which statement best describes my communication style:
   a. I can be very humorous. I sometimes have a dry sense of humor.
   b. When I speak, it is very precise and literal.
   c. My opinion is the right one.
   d. My speech is very elaborate and expressive.

9. When I'm having a bad day, my parenting style is (or would probably be):
   a. I scream and threaten but have a hard time following through on my threats. I'm too permissive and inconsistent with my discipline.
   b. Criticizing them makes children learn how to do it right. I don't believe in praising my children. They will grow up weak.
   c. I am very patient and dislike conflict. I'd rather be a bystander and let them make their own mistakes.
   d. I operate like it's a boot camp. I don't have much compassion for mistakes. Do it the right way the first time.

10. At the workplace, when I am given a project:
    a. I am a self-starter and need very little direction.
    b. I lack motivation but once I get started, I am very detail-oriented.
    c. I am precise and meticulous. I like to make lists, charts or graphs.
    d. I am easily distracted and sometimes my work is erratic.

11. My spending habits are best described as:
    a. I am very practical; I buy because of need.
    b. I look for bargains. I'm a frugal buyer.
    c. I'm an impulsive buyer.
    d. I usually buy the best.

12. When I'm attracted to someone romantically, it is usually because:
    a. They are gentle with a romantic nature. They have an appreciation for the arts and an orderly lifestyle.
    b. They are confident with strong decision-making abilities. They have a dynamic presence.
    c. They are warm, friendly and/or uninhibited.
    d. They are peaceful, easy-going and avoid conflict.

13. I'm best described as:
    a. Flexible, likeable, diplomatic, peace-loving, organized, agreeable.
    b. Spontaneous, empathetic, great encourager. I make friends easily.
    c. Self-sacrificing; dedicated friend; faithful and devoted.
    d. Independent, productive, courageous, decisive; energetic worker.

14. Careers I'm most attracted to:
    a. Builder/Contractor; President/CEO; promoter, crusader, manager, military, politician.
    b. Author, musician, physician, nurse, finish carpenter, philosopher, professor.
    c. Actor, salesperson, public relations, hairdresser, waitress.
    d. Accountant, counselor, diplomat, technician, administrator, engineer, craftsman.

15. At a wedding reception:
    a. I love being in the limelight: dancing, meeting new people, talking with as many people as I can.
    b. I feel intimidated by groups of people having fun. If I have to be there, I shy away from the crowd. I'll speak when spoken to but cannot wait for the evening to end.

- c. If an unexpected problem arises during the evening, I feel confident in finding a solution.
- d. I spend my time listening to the people seated near me or I watch the action around me.

16. I've been chosen to head up an important committee at work. During our first official meeting:
    - a. I get organized by creating lists and charts. Before the meeting is adjourned, everything on the list is discussed in detail.
    - b. I open the meeting with an ice breaker game and a few jokes. After all, no one ever said work can't be fun.
    - c. I very calmly call the meeting to order. I listen to what everyone has to say about the subject at hand. I go with the flow.
    - d. I take charge in a way that lets everyone know that I am running the show. If there is a problem I move quickly to action.

17. In the workplace:
    - a. I have little tolerance for mistakes.
    - b. I'd rather talk than work.
    - c. Not people-oriented.
    - d. Not goal-oriented.

18. The best way to get along with me is:
    - a. Learn to deal with my moodiness. Realize I am not spontaneous. Don't expect immediate answers to questions.
    - b. Don't expect me to remember appointments. Know that I am spontaneous and curious.
    - c. Don't expect enthusiasm. Remember that I dislike confrontation.
    - d. Realize that I demand respect from you. Know that I am argumentative by nature.

19. Which of these statements sound most like me:
    a. Sometimes it is hard for me to follow through.
    b. I am bored by trivia.
    c. Sometimes I find myself dwelling on negativity.
    d. Sometimes it is hard to get moving.

How to score the Four Temperaments Indicator:

Transfer all your circled answers to this test key. It tells you how many answers represent Melancholy traits; how many represent Sanguine traits; how many represent Choleric traits, and how many represent Phlegmatic traits. Count up your results in each of the four temperament categories. See which temperament you most favor. You may have a close second as well.

Legend:

Melancholy=M, Sanguine=S

Choleric=C, Phlegmatic=P

Appendices

1a. M	6a. C	11a. C	16a. M
1b. S	6b. M	11b. P	16b. S
1c. C	6c. S	11c. S	16c. P
1d. P	6d. P	11d. M	16d. C
2a. P	7a. C	12a. M	17a. C
2b. M	7b. P	12b. C	17b. S
2c. C	7c. M	12c. S	17c. M
2d. S	7d. S	12d. P	17d. P
3a. C	8a. P	13a. P	18a. M
3b. M	8b. M	13b. S	18b. S
3c. S	8c. C	13c. M	18c. P
3d. P	8d. S	13d. C	18d. C
4a. M	9a. S	14a. C	19a. S
4b. S	9b. M	14b. M	19b. C
4c. C	9c. P	14c. S	19c. M
4d. P	9d. C	14d. P	19d. P
5a. P	10a. C	15a. S	20a. C
5b. M	10b. P	15b. M	20b. M
5c. C	10c. M	15c. C	20c. P
5d. S	10d. S	15d. P	20d. S

Appendix V

Results of Phase II of the Study

Phase II of the study was conducted among the people who had participated in Phase I (the questionnaire and/or interview) and who had consented to further participate in the Preferred Sensory Mode Indicator and the Four Temperament Personality Indicator.

Phase II was done to prove and demonstrate my theory that people who primarily use their kinesthetic sensory mode (experience the world through what they feel as opposed to what they see or hear) and/or possess a Melancholy temperament, (basically introverted and introspective) are more apt to internalize abuse or what they perceive as abuse than others. These people have a harder time dealing with abuse when compared with people who lead visually or with people who favor their auditory mode, and/or possess one of the other three temperaments, (Sanguine, Phlegmatic, or Choleric).

As you read this, keep in mind the purpose of this whole project—forgiveness. It is not to see how much ammunition we can stack against the old parochial school system.

These are the results of this portion of the study:

As you recall from Appendix II, 220 of the 1000 had been molested by a member of the clergy. (If this figure seems high to you, remember human nature. The people who were more receptive to participation in the study were the ones who already took issue with the early parochial school system because of experiences of adverse treatment.)

Further, you will recall that 380 moderate or severe cases of scruples were reported. Just how many of these 220 molested people also reported scruples? Of the 220 people who were molested, 168 also reported having been plagued by scruples. This leaves 52 who, quite conceivably, hadn't internalized as much guilt, shame and fear about what had happened to them, to the point of suffering from scruples. This also means that 212 of the 380 reported cases of scruples were people who hadn't been molested at all. It had been enough for them to internalize shame, guilt and fear without a huge trauma, such as molestation in their lives.

I was able to talk with 49 of the 52 who had been molested but who hadn't internalized guilt, shame and fear to the point of suffering from scruples. Of the 49, 48 consented to take part in Phase II of the study. That is, they agreed to take the NLP Indicator which appears in Appendix III to determine what sensory mode they lead with, and the temperaments indicator in Appendix IV in order to determine their temperament. Astonishingly, none of the 48 tested as being Kinesthetic or Melancholy. Perhaps those people were not as traumatized as they would have been had they been operating in a feeling mode (Kinesthetic) and/or been prone to depression, as Melancholies are.

What about the 212 of the 380 reported cases of scruples who hadn't been molested at all? What factors contributed to their being more susceptible to internalizing guilt, shame and fear without a huge trauma in their lives? Of the 212, 152 consented to taking the sensory mode indicator and temperament indicator. All but 10 tested Kinesthetic. (These ten tested in the Visual sensory mode). But entirely all 152 profiles showed up as Melancholy temperament or a strong melancholy tendency, proving that melancholy people are much more susceptible to internalization of abuse done to them. Further, a dramatic 76% of the total people in the study who felt they were really abused in the parochial school system tested as Melancholy and Kinesthetic. Of the other 24% who reported happy memories and good times, 19% were Sanguine and the other 5% were either Choleric or Phlegmatic.

Index

A

Abandonment
  Dealing with 61
Abuse
  Emotional 46
  Intellectual 45
  Physical 42
  Sexual 43
  Spiritual 47
auditory
  Preferred Sensory Mode 14

B

Beginning Experience
  reconciliation process 7, 22
Breaking Denial, Three Steps
  Hearing Others' Stories 35
  Journaling 28
  Sharing Your Journal 35

C

Catholic bashing xiii
CDs and Downloads
  Healing Through Clearing and Cleansing the Chakras 185
  Healing Through Forgiveness of the Past 184
  Healing Through Letting Go of Negative Emotions 182
  Healing Through Manifesting the Release of Physical Pain 183
Choleric temperament 67
Cross-Addiction 83
  Religion Addicts 83
  Sex Addicts 83

D

Denial
  Three Steps to Breaking 28

E

Exercises
  Door #1 116
  Door #2 120
  Door #3 123
  Sensory Affirmation 100
  Sensory Escape 101
  Sensory Journaling 102
  Sensory Stop and Take Charge 97
  Sentence Reversal 98

F

Father Porter 37
Forgiveness
  as a Tool for Healing 5
  Your Personal Strategy for 114
Four Temperament Personality Indicator 69
Four Temperament Personality Indicator 159

H

Healing Trauma
  inner resources 93

J

Journaling 28

K

Kinesthetic
  Preferred Sensory Mode 14

L

LifeDanceTherapy©
  how it was created 178
  Mask Making 180
  what makes it unique 177
  What to Expect 179
  Who Can Benefit Most 178
  workshops 177

M

Mask Making 180
Melancholic temperament 68

N

Need to Forgive
  on an Emotional Level 112
  on a Physiological Level 110
  on a Spiritual Level 109
Negative Emotions 28
Neurolinguistic Programming
  as a communications technology xiv
  as a Modality for Forgiveness 20
  as a Modality for Remembering 16
  as a tool for forgiveness xiv 6
  Preferred Sensory Mode Indicator 153
  to Help Heal Memories 16

O

Obsessive-Compulsive Disorder 73

P

Personal Strategy
  for forgiving 114

  for remembering 112
  Understanding Connection between Remembering and Forgiving 112
Phlegmatic temperament 68
Preferred Sensory Mode
  auditory 14
  Kinesthetic 14
  visual 14
Preferred Sensory Mode Indicator 153
Preferred Sensory System
  how it can help heal 71

S

Sanguine temperament 67
Shame-based Society 79
  Toxic Shame 80
Survivors
  of physical and sexual abuse 84

T

Temperament Personality Indicator 69
The Refrigerator Game 90
Toxic Shame 80

V

Victim Sentences 96
Victim Thinking
  formula for stamping out 95
visual
  Preferred Sensory Mode 14

Y

Yearning
  as a resource for healing 50

References

Bradshaw, John. *Healing the Shame That Binds You.* Deerfield Beach, FL: Health Communications, Inc., 1988.

Catholic Encyclopedia, Vol. 14. New York: McGraw-Hill, 1967.

Fossum and Mason. *Facing Shame: Families in Recovery.* New York: W. W. Norton and Company, 1986.

Jenike, Baer, Minichiello. *Obsessive Compulsive Disorders: Theory and Management.* Littleton, Ma.: PSG Publishing Company, 1992

Jung, Carl. *The Collected Works of Carl Jung,* translated by L.F.C. Hull. NJ: Princeton University Press, Bollingen series, 1991.

Marks, I.M., M. D. *Patterns of Meaning in Psychiatric Patients.* London: Oxford University, 1965.

Wade, L .William. Relationship Discoveries, Phoenix, AZ. Personal Interview. 16 Oct. 1987.

Parlova, Gordon. Marketing Psychology, Phoenix, AZ. Personal Interview. 20 Jan. 2012.

Acknowledgments

When I first began this project in 1990, I did not realize the depth or scope of the work, nor was I cognizant of the dedication and discipline that it would demand of me.

I recognize the responsibility I have to share this work. If it lies dormant, it serves no one. It carries an important message that could not be told without the help of the following people:

It is with heartfelt gratitude that I recognize all the real champions of this story—the people who came forward to share their stories with courage and candor.

A very special thank you to the four statisticians at Ottawa University who treated the detail work of testing the validity of my Independent Study with integrity and were precise and diligent in recording the results. I honor your request to remain anonymous. Your work is greatly appreciated.

Immense gratitude goes to my editor and friend, Gordon Parlova, who added value to my work by refining points and polishing text. I appreciate your belief in my work and the dedication with which you approached the project. You wore many hats and tipped them all in the direction of my dream. Thank you for the part you played in the production of the *Healing Through* self-hypnosis series of CDs—an important derivative of this project. Your tireless efforts in the recording, mixing and editing sessions reflect your belief in me and respect for my work. I would be remiss if I did not also acknowledge your talents as a photographer. Thank you for the cover and label of the *Healing Through Letting Go of Negative Emotions* CD.

Thank you to my very gifted cover illustrator, Terry Gomez-Sandoval, who joined the project in its late stages, and after seeing a rough sketch of what I wanted, handed me an exquisite masterpiece four days later!

I want to thank Duke Getzinger, an excellent marketer and talented graphic designer, for providing the cover lay-out for the book as well as several other supporting marketing components, presented on Facebook and Twitter.

To Mark Ericson—I really value the time you took in the middle of your own demanding project to do the photo shoot that paved the way for the Facebook "group therapy session." It took a very creative eye to capture all the different "personalities." The spectacular photography that adorns the *Healing Through Manifesting the Release of Physical Pain* CD truly captures the essence of that body of work.

To Bebe Gray—educator, novelist, songwriter, friend. You helped create the impetus for me to move forward with the work I began twenty-two years ago by suggesting that "the world needs to experience your creativity, intelligence and wisdom." You're truly a catalyst for good energy! Thank you.

To Robrt Pela—Thanks for the initial editing in 1998.

Dr. John Capeccci, co-author of *Living Proof: Telling Your Story to Make a Difference*—I appreciate your support. Thanks for sharing your journey and your knowledge of the self-publishing industry.

Finally, I am completely and utterly grateful to my children: Ron, Marianna, Stephanie, Ray, Scott and Erica. You inspire me to move forward and live the life I was intended to live, learn the lessons I was meant to learn, and teach the lessons I was meant to teach.

About the Author

For twenty-eight years Dianne Pela, MA, LPC has facilitated spiritual and emotional growth in her clients through seminars, workshops and intensives. As a psychotherapist, motivational speaker, author and theorist, Ms. Pela has extensive experience in the fields of both self-help and psychotherapy. Ms Pela specializes in the following areas:

- Treatment of anxiety, depression, and bi-polar disorders
- Chemical and process addictions, including eating disorders
- Trauma, including Post Traumatic Stress Disorder (PTSD)
- Body shame/emotional shame/anger reduction
- Transactional Analysis Psychodrama
- Neurolinguistic Programming
- Grief Recovery
- Stress Management/Guided Meditations/Progressive Muscle Relaxation.

Dianne is a pioneer in utilizing Neurolinguistic Programming (NLP) as a method:

- to attain forgiveness.
- to assist in grief recovery.
- for trauma work and shame/anger reduction.
- for relapse prevention.

Ms. Pela received degrees in psychology and professional counseling from Ottawa University. She has certifications in the treatment of trauma and abuse and in chemical addictions counseling. She has worked as a Family Therapist at The Meadows Treatment Center, which is internationally renowned for the treatment of addictions and depression. Within this program, she worked with and was trained by individuals notable in the field, including Dr. Patrick Carnes, John Bradshaw, Dr. Claudia Black, and Pia Mellody. Ms. Pela then joined the professional clinical staff at Rosewood Ranch Treatment Center for Anorexia and Bulimia in Wickenburg, AZ as a Primary Therapist working exclusively with adolescent females and their families. In 1998, Dianne developed an innovative program called LifeDanceTherapy©, a division of Life Empowerment Therapy. It was while Ms. Pela was on staff at Rosewood Ranch that LifeDanceTherapy was unveiled as part of the prescribed treatment for the patients.

Ms. Pela is also the developer of *Visual Tranquility*, which is a combination of massage therapy and progressive muscle relaxation.

During her career, Dianne has orchestrated seminars and workshops throughout parts of the United States as well as in Ontario, Canada. Dianne has maintained a private practice since 2004.

"Dianne is a catalyst for good energy. She is compelling as a leader."

—Roberta Richards, PhD.

LifeDanceTherapy© Workshops

*For a list of upcoming LifeDanceTherapy© Workshops dates and times, go to www.lifeempowermenttherapy.com.

What is LifeDanceTherapy?

LifeDanceTherapy©, a division of Life Empowerment Therapy, is a trauma, shame, and anger reduction technique developed and copyrighted by Dianne M. Pela. LifeDanceTherapy© is a fresh and unique interventional approach because it combines therapeutic dance movement and Neurolinguistic Programming (NLP) to obtain therapeutic results rapidly. In most cases, dramatic results are obtained during the four-day seminar. Because of the strength and intensity with which it is presented, LifeDanceTherapy© facilitates a rapid breakthrough, allowing participants to resume—or in many cases—BEGIN a fulfilling and happy life.

What Makes LifeDanceTherapy© Unique?

Unlike any other therapeutic venue, this program combines two of the most powerful communication modalities—therapeutic dance and Neurolinguistic Programming (NLP.) As early as the 1940's, dance has been a powerful medium for therapy. Since body and mind are interrelated, therapeutic dance affects change and integrates the emotional, cognitive, and spiritual.

The concept of Neurolinguistic Programming (NLP) is simplistic. We all experience the world primarily through one of three senses—sight, sound or feeling. The sensory way in which a person is experiencing the world at any particular time is relative to how they will most effectively respond to any given therapeutic intervention.

By combining therapeutic dance and NLP, Dianne has developed a strategy that re-programs life scripts to rapidly target the troubled areas of the psyche and produce intense breakthroughs in a short period of time. To this end, the program provides the maximum benefit to people who suffer.

Who Can Benefit Most From LifeDanceTherapy©?

Certainly anyone can benefit from this method of therapy. The people who benefit most are addicts and those who suffer from any trauma including Post-Traumatic Stress Disorder (PTSD), or any body shame either alone or that which may manifest itself in conditions such as Compulsive Over-eating, Anorexia-Bulimia, or Co-Sex Addiction. This program also assists in anger management and in the reduction of shame, guilt and fear.

How LifeDanceTherapy© was Created:

In Dianne's own words:

"In February, 1985, I had taken twenty clients to a cabin in the cool pines north of Phoenix, Arizona for a weekend workshop. During the 1980's, I did a series of *Child Within* seminars and workshops. These workshops focused on family of origin work.

My participants were working hard at dumping a lot of shame and guilt from their childhood. To facilitate the process, I used my background in dance and choreography and introduced some dance techniques to promote movement of energy. At that time, I was just beginning to study NLP and decided to incorporate some of those concepts into the dance movements. The results were excellent; many of the workshop participants had major breakthroughs.

Fast forward to July, 1998. During a workshop at Ottawa University where I was a participant and not the facilitator, I was introduced to a technique for uncovering feelings that involves fashioning a paper mache' mask, using one's own face as a mold. The facilitator had used the mask-making technique as a modality with which to work on one's issues. She supported us in presenting our masks to the other participants using dance, song, poetry, or any other venue for creativity.

I took my mask home that night and placed it in front of me. I began writing a poem which turned out to be a retrospective of my life as seen through my mask persona. I then worked on a loosely scripted story of my life.

The next day, I danced out what had become a pattern in my life. During my original LifeDance, I had a major breakthrough. Even though I had scripted the life dance and knew what was coming, I had a real awakening. I knew then that I had to begin leading a *different* kind of workshop. LifeDanceTherapy© was born that day. Today's LifeDanceTherapy© is unique because it utilizes NLP and dance movement to do very delicate work very quickly. In many cases, the program takes the place of years of therapy."

What to Expect at a LifeDanceTherapy Workshop

LifeDanceTherapy© allows the flow of energy to create the impetus for growth within the therapeutic session. Both Didactic (lecture) and Experiential (hands on) exercises are featured.

At the beginning the participants are led through a series of dance and movement exercises. These exercises are geared toward elevating the level of trust among the group members. As the trust level rises, a safe environment is created which lays the groundwork for the energy work that follows. Participants begin to feel relaxed and are more comfortable telling the story of their life, through dance and movement, to the other participants.

As the workshop progresses, each participant is taught how to find and connect with their own unique strategy for releasing negative energy such as shame, anger, guilt, fear, loneliness, emotional and/or physical pain. Energy work for healing past emotional wounds and for forgiveness can also be done at this time.

During the LifeDanceTherapy© process the strategy for releasing negative emotions which allows us to heal, is based on each individual's personal style of learning. This learning style engages one or more of our main sensory modes—visual, auditory, or kinesthetic—and is one of our inner resources for healing.

Your strategy may be different than anyone else's at the workshop and unique to you. The key is finding which sensory mode for healing is your strongest, and then learning to use it for fastest results. The sensory way in which we experience the world at any particular time is relative to how we will most effectively respond to any given therapeutic intervention.

Mask Making

Many of our workshops employ the technique of Mask Making as a venue with which participants can explore their creative self as well as experience a deeper connection with their Spirit. The masks are made from gauze and a non-toxic plaster-of-Paris solution and are molded from the participant's own face. Masks are dried completely and then may be decorated ornately or simply "made up" to look exactly like the participant.

As a means of presenting the mask to the group, the participant may elect to tell the story of their life through dance and/or movement. As they do, any adverse feelings that come up are dealt with and worked through. Some participants continue to utilize the movements as a means of acting out their goals for the future. This final stage of the life dance acts as a living affirmation and can serve to facilitate life choices.

NOTE: Cost of materials for mask not included in price of workshop.

For a list of upcoming LifeDance© Workshops, Go to www.lifeempowermenttherapy.com.

**Healing Through Forgiveness of the Past Workshops are also listed on the website. These Workshops contain all the exercises and tools for forgiveness that appear within the pages of this book.

CDs and Downloads

The *Healing Through* CD Series Authored and facilitated by Dianne Pela, MA, LPC

This series of four experiential exercises combines meditation, guided imagery, autogenic training, relaxation techniques, and deep muscle relaxation with cognitive-behavioral therapy as well as self-hypnosis. These exercises also utilize the principles of Neurolinguistic Programming (NLP) to attain the fastest results, no matter if you are a visual, an auditory, or a kinesthetic learner.

"I want you to get maximum results in all areas of your life that need healing. After I created and scripted these four experiential exercises, I used them in my daily life for healing chronic physical pain, for letting go of past transgressions against me, and for letting go of negativity. So if you have any adversities in your life, this program will help you overcome them. It's about tapping into the inner resources deep inside all of us. It's just a matter of connecting to what is already within us!" –D. Pela

Healing Through Letting Go of Negative Emotions

ISBN: 978-0-9857245-2-8

ISBN: 978-0-9857245-6-6 electronic download

Negative emotions depress the immune system by blocking energy from getting to our central nervous system. Negative emotions are also stored within our bodies causing a blockage of energy flow and creating health problems. This experiential program promotes a clearing of negativity in the body. Unblock emotional pain and allow your body's energy to get to your central nervous system. This also eliminates anxiety with deep muscle relaxation and guided imagery. **Available on CD or to download.**

Go to www.lifeempowermenttherapy.com

PRODUCTS

Healing Through Manifesting the Release of Physical Pain

ISBN: 978-0-9857245-3-5

ISBN: 978-0-9857245-7-3-electronic download

Our mind is a powerful, marvelous instrument. We can overcome physical pain and heal our bodies by willing it to happen! Learn simple tools and resources that, when used on a daily basis, can lessen the intensity and even completely diminish your physical pain! **Available on CD or to download.**

Go to www.lifeempowermenttherapy.com.

Healing Through Forgiveness of the Past

ISBN: 978-0-9857245-4-2

ISBN: 978-0-9857245-8-0 electronic download

It is a universal law that when there is a forgiveness problem there is, or will be, a health problem somewhere in the physical body. This program is an experiential exercise to assist you in releasing your past and forgive yourself and others. Use this program to remove the barriers and walls you have built around your emotional wound. Ideal for use in conjunction with the book: *God Is Not a Catholic: A Recovery Journey for Adult Children of Parochial Schools.* **Available on CD or to download**

Go to www.lifeempowermenttherapy.com.

PRODUCTS

Healing Through Clearing and Cleansing the Chakras

ISBN: 978-0-9857245-5-9

ISBN: 978-0-9857245-9-7 electronic download

This exercise is designed to elevate your energy and leave you feeling more centered and balanced.
Available on CD or to download

Go to www.lifeempowermenttherapy.com.

Visit us at www.lifeempowermenttherapy.com

Follow us on Twitter: @DiannePela

Become a fan of facebook.com/GodIsNotaCatholic.

Become a fan of facebook.com/LifeEmpowermentTherapy.

Find out how to move out of the problem and into the solution.

www.ingramcontent.com/pod-product-compliance
Lightning Source LLC
Chambersburg PA
CBHW050759160426
43192CB00010B/1575